WRITERS AND THEIR WORK

ISOBEL ARMSTRONG
General Editor

BRYAN LOUGHREY
Advisory Editor

Richard II

RICHARD II AT HIS CORONATION

Panel portrait by courtesy of the Board of Trustees of the Victoria and Albert Museum

William Shakespeare

Richard II

Margaret Healy

Northcote House
in association with the
British Council

© Copyright 1998 by Margaret Healy

First published in 1998 by Northcote House Publishers Ltd,
Plymbridge House, Estover Road, Plymouth PL6 7PY, United Kingdom.
Tel: +44 (01752) 202368 Fax: +44 (01752) 202330.

British Library Cataloguing-in-Publication Data
A catalogue record for this book is available from the British Library

ISBN 0-7463-0845-0

Typeset by Kestrel Data, Exeter
Printed and bound in the United Kingdom

For John and Doreen Scott

Contents

Illustrations

Frontispiece and front cover: RICHARD AT HIS CORONATION.

Preface

Elizabeth Tudor was particularly fond of having herself painted against a backdrop of a well-tended garden. In *The Allegory of the Tudor Succession* (*c.* 1572) she is portrayed in front of a stately pleasure garden; similarly in the portrait at Welbeck Abbey (*c.* 1585) attributed to Marcus Gheeraerts (a Protestant refugee living in London), the Queen is positioned before a classical loggia and ordered knot garden, clutching an olive branch of peace. 'Tamed nature' was, in fact, symbolic of the peaceful harmonious world of Tudor England under Elizabeth's Protestant rule: woe betide anyone who alluded to its weeds! It is my contention that from behind the flimsy distancing mask of medieval history, Shakespeare did just this in *Richard II*:

> our sea-walled garden, the whole land,
> Is full of weeds, her fairest flowers chok'd up,
> Her fruit-trees all unprun'd, her hedges ruin'd,
> Her knots disordered

(III. iv. 43–6)

In the 1590s there was immense anxiety about who would succeed Elizabeth to the throne, and about her increasingly absolutist style of government. Staging discussions about 'this scept'red isle' going to seed, being disordered and badly maintained, as well as alluding to empty wombs (another touchy subject for the elderly childless queen) and portraying the deposition and the killing of an inept monarch, was inflammatory and fraught with danger – it was emphatically not a neutral or an innocent thing to do. At the time of its first performance (c. 1595), *Richard II* was deeply enmeshed in late-sixteenth-century heated political debates between those who supported royal power at whatever cost, and those who were arguing for a more limited monarchy and advocating resistance to 'tyrants'. These were the disputes, of course, that culminated in the actual deposition and killing of a king fifty years on in the English Civil War.

Today, as 400 years ago, *Richard II* remains the most politically controversial of Shakespeare's plays, and to my mind the most provocative and exciting. Interestingly, the play has the habit of inciting powerful and even ludicrous responses. Many literary critics this century have insisted that Shakespeare's play is a bastion of Tudor orthodoxy – a hymn to Tudor order and rule – in spite of the fact that the troublesome deposition scene was excised from the early printed editions of the play; that we know the play was staged on the eve of the Essex rebellion resulting in the cross-examination in the dock of one of the players; in spite of all the topical allusions in the play which were unfavourable to Elizabeth's regime; that we know Elizabeth felt herself to have been extensively cloned by her detractors to her troublesome forebear, Richard II; and in spite of the fact that it was banned as subversive by Charles II. Other critics have argued – equally irrationally – that the play has virtually no political remit at all, and that it is all about Richard's tragic nature. It was perhaps inevitable, given these extreme responses, that this play would become deeply embroiled in late-twentieth-century controversies about the political allegiances of the nation's Bard. Is he an upholder of the status quo – a propagandist for the Tudor regime – or a more questioning, radical, even subversive playwright? *Richard II* is a key text over which the battle between right- and left-wing critics for the political body of the Bard has been, and still is being fought. Whilst I hope it is clear throughout this book which colours I fly, my intention has been to muster all the relevant evidence so that the reader can join the camp of his or her choice. To this end, I have taken the unusual step of relegating the history chronicles to the margins of the discussion (where they belong), re-situating Shakespeare's play back firmly amidst the sixteenth-century humanist political debates which echo through the playtext, and which I believe provide us with invaluable but neglected insights into how the play may have functioned at its original moment of production.

Engaging in an exhaustive and relentless exploration of the tangled interrelations between politics, history, language, morality and power relations, *Richard II* is a play which, more than any other in the canon, seems to anticipate the postmodern condition experienced in the academy today as a registering of doubt in relation to old epistemological frameworks, as a quest for new theoretical approaches, for new meaning – what is history; what is the nature of words; what is it that determines gender; how is power maintained by authority? This quest for meaning necessitates an exchange with the past – to make sense of the present we inevitably reflect back. Through a thorough historicizing approach, and through adopting and explaining recent theoretical perspectives on Shakespeare's play, I hope I have succeeded in bringing a small but important piece of the past into a meaningful dialogue with us today.

Acknowledgements

I am extremely grateful to Isobel Armstrong for providing me with the opportunity to write about *Richard II* – a play which has long intrigued me. I would like to thank Helen Hackett for commenting on my early grapplings with the text, and Tom Healy for reading drafts of the manuscript and succouring me along the way to its completion. Finally, I would like to thank all the members of The London Renaissance Seminar, but especially Sue Wiseman, Alan Stewart, Sasha Roberts, Michelle O'Callaghan and Gordon McMullen, for years of stimulating debate which I am sure has informed, and helped shape, this little book.

Note on the Text

Shakespearean references are to the Arden edition of individual plays throughout.

Spelling of primary texts has not been modernized beyond the usual conventions of transforming 'v' to 'u', 'i' to 'j', and so forth.

Abbreviations and References

1 Henry IV	*Henry IV, Part I*
2 Henry IV	*Henry IV, Part 2*
An Homilie	*An Homilie Against disobedience and wilfull rebellion*
The Institution	*The Institution of Christian Religion*
OED	*Oxford English Dictionary*

1

Political Voices

'TELL THOU THE LAMENTABLE TALE OF ME' (V. i. 44)

> I am a kyng that ruled all by lust,
> That forced not of vertue, ryght, or lawe,
> But alway put false Flatterers most in trust
> . . . .
> What pleasure prykt, that thought I to be just,
> I set my minde, to feede, to spoyle, to just.
>
> (William Baldwin, *A Myrroure For Magistrates*, 1559)[1]

He . . . beganne to rule by will more than by reason, threatning deathe to eche one that obeyed not his inordinate desires. (Raphael Holinshed, *Chronicles*, 1577)[2]

Richard's 'tale' was as notorious as it was 'lamentable': by the late sixteenth century when Shakespeare wrote *The Tragedy of King Richard the Second*, the story of this young monarch's unpropitious rule had achieved legendary status. Time and again English poems and chronicles had reiterated Richard's excesses: his love of flattery, his disregard of good counsel, his flouting of the law, his lust, greed and partiality for fashionable clothing (he is said to have invented the handkerchief). Indeed, a poem survives, entitled *Richard the Redeless* (counsel-less) c. 1399, which reveals that even before his death Richard's 'lamentable tale' had been incorporated into the 'advice to princes' (or 'mirror for princes') genre to warn 'every Cristen kyng that ony croune bereth', who follows his own pleasures rather than wisdom, against making the same mistakes as this king of 'misrule'. This Middle English poem represents Henry Bolingbroke's successes as divinely engineered ('The lord of heaven rose in His righteous anger against evil-doers in royal array'): King Richard was 'rightfully' deposed because he had wilfully disregarded the welfare of his subjects.[3] Indeed, casting Richard as the tyrannical villain of the piece,

Richard the Redeless evinces no doubts that God was on the side of the Lancastrian Henry IV; but there are also a few anti-Lancastrian chronicles, mostly in French and very much a minority, which depict a rather different scenario, comparing Richard's sufferings with those of Christ and his judges with Pilate, and predicting divine vengeance on his behalf. Shakespeare's play invokes both versions of Richard's history and through the use of devices like the mirror episode (IV. i), and the verbally self-reflexive 'tale of me', it wittily and self-consciously identifies itself as yet another 'mirror for princes', telling the story of a prince who reveals himself to have been steeped in this pedagogic genre designed to inculcate the principles of good government in rulers, though, ironically, with no obvious profit either for himself or his country – indeed, quite the reverse. Furthermore, through bringing the two interpretations of Richard's life into startling and unsettling collision (Richard the tyrant and Richard the martyr), the play inevitably raises questions about writing the past, foregrounding 'history' as a narrative which frequently occludes social conflicts. Shakespeare's *Richard II* is, thus, no static morality play or pale reflection of history: through dramatizing an unusually hybrid and problematized tale of Richard, it simultaneously engages with the political debates of its time about just rule and its opposite, and wryly pokes fun at the rhetorical play of ideology and the displays of political power which it enacts.

In order to illustrate these points it is necessary to re-situate Shakespeare's work in the historical and cultural location which gave birth to it; and to re-establish the intertextual network within which it exists, for texts are porous, and open to the mutual intertextual influences of one another. It is this porosity which ensures that, in the new historicist Stephen Greenblatt's terms, literary creations are linked to 'the complex network of institutions, practices, and beliefs that constitute the culture as a whole'.[4] The posited historical 'sources' for Shakespeare's *Richard II* have been repeatedly documented by successive editors; indeed, the voices of the contemporary historiographers Raphael Holinshed, Samuel Daniel, and Edward Hall are so loud in the critics' discussions that they have tended to drown out important other intertextual echoes;[5] echoes which reveal this play to be deeply embedded in sixteenth-century controversies between champions of royal absolutism, and those who favoured a more 'limited monarchy checked and lessened by aristocracy and democracy'.[6] Let me try to tune in to some of the submerged yet highly significant political 'voices' reverberating through this extremely polyvalent playtext.

'T'UNDECK THE POMPOUS BODY OF A KING' (IV. i. 250): THE HUMANIST 'MIRRORS' AND SHAKESPEARE'S RICHARD II

> If a necklace, a scepter, royal robes, a train of attendants are all that make a king, what is to prevent the actors who come on the stage decked with all the pomp of state from being called king? What is it that distinguishes a real king from an actor? It is the spirit befitting a prince. (Erasmus, *The Education of a Christian Prince*, 1516)[7]

Shortly before taking up his appointment in 1516 as the tutor to the future King Charles V, the foremost Northern Renaissance humanist, Erasmus of Rotterdam, sat down at his desk in a state of extreme disillusionment with Europe's rulers, and penned a treatise of instruction for 'Christian Princes' (a 'mirror for princes') which was to have a profound impact on humanist political debates for well over a century. He wrote to Sir Thomas More with news of his project and the latter revealingly replied: 'How I wish Christian princes would follow good instructions. Everything is upset by their mad follies. I am very desirous of having this book, for I am sure that like everything else of yours it will turn out perfect.'[8] Erasmus's authority was by this time sufficiently well established to allow him to give a candid assessment of what he saw as the root cause of the wars and moral corruption which (in his estimation) were tearing the continent of Europe and the Christian Church to pieces – foolish and tyrannical, 'beastly' princes. Europe's princes appeared to Erasmus to have become bloody warlords, 'plagues to the world' milking their subjects for taxes in order to satisfy their tyrannical appetites. Many times *The Education of a Christian Prince* laments how the ways of 'some princes' had slipped back to such a point that the two ideas of 'good man' and 'prince' seemed 'to be the very antithesis of one another'. It meticulously analyses the meaning and duties of kingship, insisting on the Platonic dictum that only those of the 'highest moral integrity' with their bodily passions fully under the control of reason (models of 'frugality and temperance'), who put the interests and offices of the state before their own pleasures, are fit to govern; others are 'sham' princes – mere actors decked out with symbolic regalia. Europe's philosopher-kings of the future must be rigorously disciplined from childhood: any tyrannical tendencies must be 'weeded out' by the tutor-gardener at their earliest signs. The prince's obligation to exercise proper management of his own body and soul is matched by the need to scrutinize the body of the kingdom, and, like a physician, to diagnose and cure its diseases: 'What is the prince but the physician of the state?'[9]

In fact Erasmus's treatise skilfully deconstructs the meaning of kingship, insisting that it has nothing to do with the trappings and titles of monarchy: 'What does the anointing of the king mean, unless the greatest mildness of spirit? What significance has the crown on his head, if not the wisdom that is absolute?'; and stressing that the 'ruling power' of a Christian state consists only of 'administration, kindness and protection'. Of tyrants, the text rails: 'If you strip them of their royal ornaments and inherited goods, and reduce them to themselves alone, you will find nothing left except the essence of an expert at dice . . . and every other kind of crime'. By contrast, the virtuous prince 'will be great even if his princely authority is stripped from him'. Such constructions set out, of course, to challenge the notion of the inherited, divine right of 'bad' kings to rule; to expose the fabricated character of the political order and the threatricality, the role playing, implicit in power brokering. Having provided lengthy portraits of both the virtuous prince and his 'actor' antithesis, the treatise is explicit about the drastic action which the latter type should take on recognizing his unsatisfactory image in this 'mirror': 'If these conditions are not to your liking, why do you desire the burden of ruling? Or if you inherited this authority, why do you not yield it to another?' Twice *The Education of a Christian Prince* exhorts the bad prince to 'yield' his authority to 'one who meets the requirements you should have'; and many times it warns of the dire consequences of not relinquishing power and subsequently of making 'a farce' of 'the laws of Christ', of vaunting 'under the glory of Christ as a pretext': 'There is but one death for all – beggars and kings alike. But the judgment after death is not the same for all. None are dealt with more severely than the powerful'.[10] Erasmus's gloss in his *Paraphrases* (1548) to the biblical passage 'it is more easy for a camel to go through the iye of a nedle, than for a riche man to enter the kyngdome of heaven' (Luke 18:25) is a variation on the same theme: 'For so he reproved the covetous riche man, unto whom riches be rather a burden, than profit which they bear for others rather than themselves'.[11] Beggars, kings, and this very text are, of course, the things that Shakespeare's much chastened Richard anxiously ruminates on in his prison cell (V. v. 1–66).

Keeping Erasmus's dictums about princely behaviour in mind, let us turn now to consider the 'woeful pageant' scene of Shakespeare's play (IV. i), which begins with York interrupting the rather farcical Parliamentary gage-throwing interlude (see ch. 3, p.35) to relay the shocking news of Richard's decision to 'yield' his authority to another. Any residual laughter is stilled, the mood in the auditorium changes to one of extreme gravity as York drops his bombshell:

> Great Duke of Lancaster, I come to thee
> From plume-pluck'd Richard, who with willing soul
> Adopts thee heir, and his high sceptre yields
> To the possession of thy royal hand.
>
> (IV. i. 107–10)

Bolingbroke responds unhesitatingly, 'In God's name, I'll ascend the regal throne' (l. 113), and notwithstanding Carlisle's indignant explosion about an anointed king, the 'figure of God's majesty' (l. 125) being displaced, Richard is summoned

> To do that office of thine own good will
> Which tired majesty did make thee offer:
> The resignation of thy state and crown
> To Henry Bolingbroke.
>
> (IV. i. 177–80)

In Shakespeare's play, Richard 'yields', 'resigns', and finally undoes himself ('I will undo myself', IV. i. 203) in an inversion of a coronation ceremony which involves his publicly divesting himself of the ornaments, trappings and titles of kingship – undecking 'the pompous body of a king' (l. 250) – revealing 'Proud majesty a subject' (l. 252); and 'unkinged' Richard, stripped of his princely authority, finds himself exposed as a sham and worse, in the eyes of many observing this 'woeful pageant' (l. 321), a criminal. Invoking the contrasting, more favourable, interpretation of events, alluding to himself as Christ and his detractors as Pilates, Richard proceeds to threaten the assemblage with his anointed status: 'water cannot wash away your sin' (l. 242). Finally he sends for a mirror to review his image – 'bankrupt of his majesty' (l. 267) – declaring that there he will

> read enough
> When I do see the very book indeed
> Where all my sins are writ . . .
>
> (IV. i. 273–5)

The mirror episode is rich with suggestive meaning (see ch. 3, pp. 44–7), but it is tempting to speculate that one perspective alluded to here is Erasmus's 'mirror', a book in which all the sins of the tyrant prince masquerading 'under the glory of Christ as a pretext' are laid bare in a remarkably immediate and theatrical manner.[12] Interestingly, none of the reputed historical sources of this play describe Richard 'yielding' his authority to his successor – something which has perplexed many commentators.

Yet it was not necessary for Shakespeare to have read *The Education of a Christian Prince* to have been aware of Erasmus's arguments, or, indeed, of the dramatic style in which they were presented: *The Praise of Folly*, the *Adages* and the *Colloquies* – more widely disseminated Erasmian texts – all contain very similar expositions of the Christian prince and his tyrannical opposite emphasizing the 'play' of power. Shortly after the publication of *The Education of a Christian Prince*, English humanists were extolling its pedagogic virtues. Laurence Humphrey's detailed account of the best instruction for a young nobleman emphasized this as a seminal text to inculcate desired behaviour: 'Reade he also all wryters of Nobilitie. Erasmus of the Institution of a Christian Prince . . . In them as mirrours, to see and beholde hym selfe' (1563).[13] Juin Luis Vives recommended it as essential reading after Plato's *Republic*, and likewise Sir Thomas Elyot. Indeed, Elyot's *The Book Named the Governor* (1531), which became the most widely read English book of instruction for would-be 'governors' (undergoing eight editions before 1580), is heavily indebted to its acknowledged Erasmian model. Although Elyot avoided dabbling his toes in the dangerous waters of tyranny stirred up by Erasmus, he warned his governor that the 'weighty or heavy cloak' of authority would 'shortly be taken of him that did put it thee, if thou use it negligently', insisting that rulers were first and foremost men with no more of 'the dew of heaven, or the brightness of the sun, than any other person'. Echoing Erasmus he cautioned: 'do also remember that in nothing only in virtue ye are better than another inferior person'. Elyot agreed that the 'excesses' to which rulers were prone had to be kept in check through the exercise of temperance with strict adherence to the bounds of mediocrity, 'to keep desire under the yoke of reason'.[14] In the manner of Plato's *Republic*, both these humanist 'mirrors' illustrate their philosophical points abundantly through analogies drawn from the body, medicine, husbandry and music.

All the plays in Shakespeare's Lancastrian sequence (*Richard II, 1* and *2 Henry IV, Henry V*) share both this imagistic base, and the concerns of these humanist advice books with the dangers of 'excess' at the top. Indeed, they depict a kingdom grievously diseased through a monarch's 'surfeit'. As the Archbishop of York describes the malady in *2 Henry IV*:

> we are all diseas'd,
> And with our surfeiting, and wanton hours,
> Have brought ourselves into a burning fever,
> And we must bleed for it; of which disease
> Our late King Richard being infected died.

> (IV. i. 54–8)

In essence the plays depict a version of this Erasmian nightmare:

> The corruption of an evil prince spreads more swiftly and widely than the scourge of any pestilence . . . under an epicure, all disport in wasteful luxury; under a debauchee, licence is rampant . . . no comet . . . affects the progress of human affairs as the life of the prince grips and transforms the morals and character of his subjects.[15]

Richard's personal disorder ('His rash fierce blaze of riot', II. i. 33, 'Light vanity', II. i. 38, 'profane hours', V. i. 25) is like a contagion, producing an epidemic of surfeit and corruption in his kingdom. Indeed, measured against the exactions of the advice books, Richard gets everything wrong: he is no physician, he is a bad husbandman of his land, he resents the care of his office, he dislikes the Commons and overburdens them with taxes, he disregards the law. Bolingbroke, the usurper, is a marked improvement on his princely predecessor, yet he is guilty by proxy of the 'excess' of murder: his style of regiment proves inadequate to restore health to the commonwealth which remains a 'beastly feeder' (2 *Henry IV*, I. iii. 95). It is only under the brief rule of the self-styled philosopher-king Henry V ('We are no tyrant, but a Christian king', *Henry V*, I. ii. 241), who understands the office of king, and who recognizes and is in control of his own human fallibility ('I think the king is but a man, as I am . . . his ceremonies laid by, in his nakedness he appears but a man' (*Henry V*, IV. i. 101–6), that the monarch's subjects are full of 'duty and zeal'. Echoing the tenets of Erasmian humanism on the 'right' behaviour of a Christian prince, and self-consciously prizing his 'inward true and duteous spirit' above his regalia (*Henry IV*, IV. v. 147), Harry appears truly – in deeds as well as words – 'Twin-born with greatness' (2 *Henry V*, IV. i. 240).

In his influential book *The King's Two Bodies*, the historian Ernst Kantorowicz made the case that 'The image of the twinned nature of a king', was distinctively Shakespearean (his 'own and proper vision'), though inspired by Edmund Plowden's legal terminology (Plowden was an Elizabethan jurist).[16] The concept of 'the king's two bodies' – his natural body and his office (body politic) – was, however, already well developed in the humanist advice books of the early sixteenth century, which were the most popular branch of political literature in the Renaissance; and, as we have seen, the substance of these 'mirrors' seems to have been very familiar to the playwright. These ideas were developed to form the basis of a radical humanist political philosophy, and widely disseminated in the second half of the century; and it was undoubtedly the currency and topicality of these debates which made them promising material for the commercial theatre in the 1590s. In order to understand the politics of *Richard II*, therefore, it is necessary to grapple further with humanist theories of the proper regiment of princes which by the 1560s had embarked on a collision course with Tudor orthodoxy.

It is noteworthy that whilst Erasmus and Thomas Elyot stressed temperance and moderation as essential princely attributes, neither suggested deposition as a viable alternative to suffering the excesses of a sinful monarch. Undoubtedly they would have agreed with John Calvin's pronouncement in *The Institution of*

Christian Religion that the correction of 'unbridled government' was the 'revengemente of the Lorde, [therefore] let us not by and by thynke that it is committed to us, to whom there is geven no other commaundement but to obey and suffer'.[17] In the early days of religious reform, Luther, Calvin and Tyndale had all preached the Christian obligation of obedience to rulers, but the reverses which the Protestant movement experienced from the 1540s no doubt shook the faith of the reformers in the efficacy of passive obedience. With English Protestantism in danger of being all but eradicated an increasingly militant doctrine of resistance was promulgated, particularly by the reformers forced into exile by Mary I's Catholic regime of 1553–8, and the Scottish Presbyterians, the latter having to justify their part in the forced abdication of Mary Queen of Scots. John Knox's polemics against the latter, for example, represent the corruption and inordinate appetites of princes as being bound up with allegiance to the Roman Church: actively to resist such rulers is to obey God and his justice.

After 1559 Calvin added a passage to *The Institution* which similarly set obedience to 'the ordinance of God' against the rule of 'the outraging licentiousnesse of Kinges'. The 'office' of 'Magistrates for the behalfe of the people' obliged their concerted action against tyrannical rulers: 'if they winke at Kinges wilfully raging over and treading down the poore communaltie, their dissembling is not without wycked breache of faith'.[18] 'Faith' – Protestantism – now involved protecting the liberty of the people against 'raging', unbridled kings. Calvinist doctrine was subsequently considerably at variance with that set out in the Elizabethan homilies and read in all churches every Sunday, which maintained that political insurrection ('rebellion') against a monarch was 'worse than the worst government of the worst prince'.[19]

George Buchanan, humanist tutor to young James VI of Scotland, developed both these strands of Protestant thought in his important treatise, *The Powers of the Crown in Scotland* (1579), which formed a considerable basis for later Puritan political theory. Deemed subversive, this text was officially banned in England although the ideas it contained probably achieved fairly wide circulation: in *The Defence of Poesy*, Sir Philip Sidney admired Buchanan's plays, which dramatized his political theories, and we know that Ben Jonson owned a copy of the suppressed treatise.

Buchanan insisted on the Ciceronian principle that no person in a state was above the law which the people, through their representatives, enacted; this necessarily entailed a collision with the doctrine that sovereignty was inherited, divine, and therefore not subject to earthly sanctions – the divine right of kings to rule. Like Erasmus, Buchanan stressed the dual nature of kingship: 'the ruler is not a king only, but is as well, a man . . . He is, in fact, an animal'; but he proceeded to assert the ethicacy of the deposition of 'beastly' rulers, and of executing 'vengeance on an arrogant and worthless tyrant'.[20] In fact the confrontation between two theories of government – one based on inherited right and the other on office – which is so evident in Buchanan's tract, was destined to remain centre stage and formed the political dividing line in the dispute between Royalists and Parliamentarians in the English Civil War. Imprisoned in the Tower, Sir John Strangeways, the royalist member of Parliament wrote in 1647: 'We maintayne that the king is king by inhaerent birth-right; they say his kingly power is an office upon trust'.[21] It is firmly amidst this late-sixteenth- and seventeenth-century war of ideas between advocates of resistance to tyrants and champions of absolute monarchy that Shakespeare's *Richard II* should be situated.

DISEASE IN EDEN: THE RHETORIC OF IDEOLOGY

> I will use the policy of a wise and cunning gardener (*The Book Named the Governor*, p. 15)

Whilst a few literary critics have noted the presence of verbal echoes from Thomas Elyot's *The Book Named the Governor* in Shakespeare's Lancastrian plays, the resonances and parallels from its more radical humanist relations (including Erasmus's 'mirror') have rather surprisingly – given *Richard II*'s shared concerns and imagistic base – been unduly neglected. The language of disease, humoral medicine, and husbandry, pervades the Lancastrian history plays in a particularly organic and unrelenting manner which should, indeed, serve to highlight their participation in the sixteenth-century political debates outlined above. Buchanan, for example, expounds his theories in *The Powers of The Crown in Scotland* through a pronounced body-centred logic of proper regimen which the Lancastrian sequence shares:

Both the human body and the body-politic are injured by the presence in them of harmful things and by the lack of things they need. Each body is cured in much the same way as the other – namely, by nourishing and gently assisting the weakened members and by diminishing the fullness and excess of that which does no good.[22]

At first such medical correspondences seem commonplace and innocuous, but Buchanan's democratic philosophy proceeds to carry this balancing-act logic to an extreme which eventually justifies the eradication of particularly top-heavy elements within the body politic – monarchs given to excesses. Indeed, when he was writing this tract, Mary Stuart was in the process of being radically excised from the body politic on the basis of such reasoning.

For Buchanan, order within the body politic of a fallen, degenerate world prone to diseases was not a natural, normal given, but a hard-worn condition:

> Now, just as in human bodies, composed as they are of conflicting elements, there are diseases . . . so, of necessity, the men associated in these bodies which we call states are of diverse and often of opposing sorts . . . It is certain, in short, that they would separate and go to ruin, unless there were a physician to cure diseases.[23]

In this treatise, discord of elements within the social body is the regrettable but normal tendency, and 'ruin' of the state can only be averted through sound government guided by reason, and timely 'cures'.

A similar ordering incentive and humoral model informs Shakespeare's gardener's practice of husbandry as well as his political reflections: constant vigilance and skill are required to cultivate the post-Edenic garden which is naturally given to over-profusion and unruliness. This radical husbandman who voices democratic sentiments – 'even . . . government' (III. iv. 36) – notably, however, has no hesitation in instructing his helper to imitate 'an executioner' and: 'Cut off the heads of too fast growing sprays,/That look too lofty in our commonwealth' (III. iv. 34–5). There is no gardener in Buchanan's treatise but gardening analogies abound in both Erasmus's and Elyot's tracts and a 'wise and cunning' gardener-counsellor features in the latter. Their gardeners, though, engage in notably more gentle strategies of

11

husbandry, preparing ground and weeding – no lopping off heads here. Shakespeare's shrewd but knife-happy gardener – 'Superfluous branches/We lop away' (III. iv. 63–4) – would certainly not have been welcomed as a political adviser in Erasmus's or Elyot's commonwealths, or even in Buchanan's, though Machiavelli might have countenanced him. Indeed, in his advocacy of merciless political expediency the democratic gardener is, in fact, counselling tyranny.

It is possible that some among the play's original audiences would have detected an oblique criticism of Elizabeth I's style of government here: in the late 1560s Elizabeth had written a political poem couched in the rhetoric of husbandry ('the toppe of hope supprest the roote upreard shalbe/and fruictles all there grafted guile') which threatened her cousin Mary Stuart with execution should she grow too proud and ambitious: 'my rustye sword throwghe rest shall first his eydge imploye/to poule there toppes that sekes suche chaunge or gape for future joye.'[24] In the event Mary languished in prison – rather chastened we may assume – for nineteen years until in 1587 Elizabeth deemed it timely to 'poule' her 'toppe'. George Puttenham published Elizabeth's poem in *The Arte of English Poesie* in 1589, commending it, rather ironically, as 'most sweet and sententious'. In the 1590s any dissatisfied jibes at the monarch's increasing absolutism had to be made with Aesopian indirection (animal fables associated with Aesop often disguised political comment) so we should not dismiss such resonances in stage plays lightly. Whether or not Shakespeare's fallen Eden scene was infused with more particularized political comment, *Richard II* certainly encouraged its audience both to weigh up the strategies and ethics of opposing political philosophies (democratic and absolutist),[25] and to be wary of 'cunning' extremists whose densely figurative and captivating rhetoric might, indeed, conceal worse, or similar, excesses to those they railed against.

It should be recalled at this juncture how Shakespeare's arch-political strategist, Richard Gloucester, had sought to tarnish the reputation of the king by insinuating his intemperance: 'O, he hath kept an evil diet long,/And over-much consum'd his royal person' (*Richard III*, I. i. 139–40). In 1 and 2 *Henry IV* the character most obsessed with his own physical constitution and with medical name dropping – Falstaff – is the one who is least self-governed and who is prepared, as Richard Gloucester had been, to turn 'diseases to commodity' (2 *Henry IV*, I. ii. 250). In fact, in the Lancastrian sequence, images of oral gluttedness (and their opposite which produces lean Gaunt) are everywhere in excessive profusion and, deployed to a logical but ridiculous extreme, they function inevitably to weaken the authority of the language of dietary regimen (which is effectively parodied), and ultimately of the potent medical rhetoric so cherished by the humanist politicians.

AN OPEN TEXT

If Shakespeare's play encourages a heightened sceptical consciousness in the face of the persuasive political rhetoric its voices deploy, it simultaneously refuses to authorize any of those voices, ultimately plunging its audience into a sea of ethical quandary. It is the troublesome linkage of Richard's 'anointed' status with what Holinshed termed his 'inordinate desires' which produces the dilemmas about justice which the play enacts. Let us examine the text's skilful manipulation of its contending voices rather more closely.

Richard's noble uncles, Gaunt and York, recognize and disapprove of his 'surfeit', yet they are paralysed to do anything to impede their country's decline, or, indeed, to revenge their brother's death, because they believe that 'God's is the quarrel' (I. ii. 37); and, like Richard, that 'heaven still guards the right' (III. ii. 62). The impotence of these elder statesmen in the face of injustice and impending national chaos exposes the shallowness of orthodox Tudor political doctrine which is expounded most fully in this play by the Bishop of Carlisle. He asks 'What subject can give sentence on his king?' (IV. i. 121) – a question posed and answered by Buchanan in his treatise – and proceeds:

> And shall the figure of God's majesty,
> His captain, steward, deputy elect,
> Anointed, crowned, planted many years,
> Be judg'd by subject and inferior breath . . .

(IV. i. 125–8)

The shoring up of the abuses of absolutism with what Erasmus described as 'pagan terms', like 'majesty', would not have met with Erasmus's approval. Even the more conservative Thomas Elyot challenged assumptions about a ruler's divine status, as we have seen. Buchanan, however, went considerably further; he brazenly outfaced the Tudor dogma, offering a contrasting perspective:

> God, as has been said before, orders evil persons put out of the way; nor does he except any rank, or sex, or condition, or person whatsoever; and kings have from him no consideration that is denied to beggars.[26]

Buchanan's may be taken as an extreme view, yet it was an influential one especially in militant Protestant circles. It is probable that some among *Richard II*'s original audiences would have greeted Carlisle's pronouncements with a degree of scepticism, and on the eve of the Essex rebellion (see ch. 2) they might even have hissed and booed.

Richard's uncle York, acknowledged by him as 'just', functions in this play to foreground and challenge the King's unlawful seizing of 'Herford's rights' (II. i. 201), and to highlight Bolingbroke's trespass in braving arms against his sovereign. He becomes the voice of care-worn authority charged with an ethical and legal dilemma which he cannot resolve:

> Both are my kinsmen:
> Th' one is my sovereign, whom both my oath
> And duty bids defend; th'other again
> Is my kinsman, whom the King hath wrong'd,
> Whom conscience and my kindred bids to right.

> (II. ii. 111–15)

Giving the appearance of a bumbling coward as much as a dutiful subject and governor, York determines to do nothing ('remain as neuter', II. iii. 158) except fall back on God and let him settle the quarrel which Bolingbroke eventually wins. The audience is left to speculate whether God has determined Bolingbroke's success (as the latter claims and York chooses to believe), or whether the usurper is opposing God's justice whilst invoking his authority. A comparable conflict to York's, between 'oath' and 'conscience', was destined to exercise the minds of duteous Englishmen throughout the Stuart reign: only by installing divinity firmly in human conscience and divesting the king's majesty of it could the ethical dilemma be sufficiently resolved to open the way for legal action against an absolutist-style monarch.

Shakespeare notably uses the rather unreliable bully, Northumberland, as the mouthpiece of the Buchanan-style law of the people; he demands, giving Richard papers:

> you read
> These accusations, and these grievous crimes
> Committed by your person and your followers
> Against the state and profit of this land;
> That, by confessing them, the souls of men
> May deem that you are worthily depos'd.

(IV. i. 222–7)

Whether or not Richard has been 'worthily depos'd' (or whether in fact he has yielded his authority, or been unworthily deposed) is not resolved by the playtext, and the confusing scenario which ensues, centring on the question of which king is the legitimate monarch – the anointed one, or his successor who commands the Commons' support – is not resolved either; even the two kings are unsure about it. Whilst Bolingbroke is riddled with guilt and anxiety that he has, in fact, opposed God's will, Richard's words reflect his genuine puzzlement: 'God save the king! although I be not he;/And yet, amen, if heaven do think him me' (IV. i. 174–5).

Does sovereignty exist in 'care' (office), in a crown, in a name, in popular support, in an anointed body? Are events determined by Providence, Fortune, or by mere mortals invoking deities for their own ends? Were the civil wars of Henry IV's reign divine punishment for his opposing of God's ordinance, or the legacy of Richard's 'surfeit'? Can a bad, yet anointed king 'yield' his authority to another as Erasmus suggested he should? The Elizabethan audience was left pondering a variety of contestatory perspectives, and in an ethical and philosophical quandary which anticipated the political dilemma of some fifty years hence, and which could, in the end, only be settled by an appeal to individual conscience and reason.

Richard II, is, thus, a remarkably open text which interrogates the meaning of kingship, and which dramatizes and exposes the limitations and pitfalls both of the orthodox Tudor line on monarchy which could function to sustain tyranny, and of the humanist debates which, at their most extreme, countenanced the deposition and even the killing of kings. Functioning as a site of debate and dissension – an occasion for the jostling of orthodox and heterodox impulses – the playtext offers no clear-cut, uncomplicated solutions to the problems it poses. Given this indeterminacy, the theatrical realization of the text (its interpretation by the players) and the circumstances of performance (such as the staging of it on the eve of the Essex rebellion), might considerably affect the play's political implications and impact.

2

Shaping History

'FROM THE STAGE TO THE STATE': DRAMA'S 'POWER TO
SUBVERT'

> On Thursday or Friday sevennight, Sir Chas. Percy, Sir Josceline Percy,
> Lord Monteagle, and several others spoke to some of the players to
> play the deposing and killing of King Richard II, and promised to give
> them 40s. more than their ordinary, to do so. Examinate and his fellows
> had determined to play some other play, holding that of King Richard
> as being so old and so long out of use that they should have a small
> company at it, but at this request they were content to play it. (State
> Papers. Dom. Eliz. 1598–1601)[1]

On the Thursday or Friday before the Essex rebellion of Sunday,
8 February 1601, a number of the Earl of Essex's men, including
his steward Gilly Meyricke, sought out members of the Lord
Chamberlain's company and offered them twice as much money
as they would normally earn to perform an out-of-date play,
almost certainly Shakespeare's *Richard II*, on the next Saturday
afternoon. The unlucky bargain was struck and, on the day prior
to the uprising, eleven of the conspirators dined together before
crossing the Thames and making their way to the Globe to feast
their eyes on what Sir Francis Bacon later described as 'that
tragedie which hee [Meyricke] thought soone after his lord should
bring from the stage to the state'.[2] The plot to depose Queen
Elizabeth and replace her with the Earl of Essex, however, failed,
and a representative of Shakespeare's troop – the actor, Augustine
Phillips – shortly found himself in the dock being questioned
about the company's seditious activities – the staging of *Richard
II* on the eve of a rebellion.

This narrative, put together from trial documents and Francis
Bacon's pamphlet of 1601 detailing the event,[3] sits uneasily with
attempts made earlier this century by influential critics like E. M.
W. Tillyard and John Dover Wilson to represent Shakespeare's
play as a bastion of Tudor orthodoxy which basically set out to

reinforce the message of the Homilies stressing 'what an abomin-
able sinne agaynst God and man rebellion is'. Dover Wilson went
so far as to proclaim that all Elizabethans were so grateful for
their 'deliverance' from the Wars of the Roses that they considered
the House of Tudor 'the saviour of England'; furthermore:

> The constitution in which they rejoiced was not a democracy . . . with
> . . . the paraphernalia of parliamentary government, but a monarchy
> . . . a monarchy divinely ordained, strong, absolute, unchallenged, and
> entirely popular. To them the blessings of the Tudor government were
> so patent, so unquestionable that their only fear was lest something
> should arise to threaten its permanence or supremacy.[4]

In Dover Wilson's doctrinaire view, all Englishmen in their right
mind, including Shakespeare, worshipped the notion of order and
would, therefore, with no hesitation, have pronounced Bolingbroke a dangerous 'usurper'. This 'hymn to Tudor Order', as it
has since been appropriately dubbed, held important though by
no means uncontested sway for many years until the conservative,
authoritarian ideology underlying it was exposed and taken
severely to task in the 1980s by a new breed of radical, politicized
scholars intent on breaking the right's stronghold over the canon.
Since then the major exponents of the 'Tudor myth' (its other
negative designation) have received regular, repetitive critical
beatings from the left; whilst representatives of the more orthodox,
liberal-humanist wing of criticism have responded with volleys of
shot aimed at undermining the methodology and assumptions of
the new historicism.

Indeed, in many ways *Richard II* qualifies as a key text over
which the battle for the political ownership of Renaissance literature has been (and still is being) fought. This is undoubtedly
because incontrovertible evidence exists (in the form of the
documents surrounding the Essex rebellion) which establishes the
potential of this play to intervene in and influence the outcome
of events beyond the theatre: a potential noted implicitly in Francis
Bacon's contemporary phraseology – 'from the stage to the state'
– and which was latched onto eagerly by historicist critics of the
left. Here was evidence that the Renaissance stage did more than
simply mirror reality (as earlier criticism assumed); it helped shape
it, constituting one of the creative forces of history. Consider the
assertions made in two introductions to ground-breaking volumes

by the new historicist and cultural materialist critics Stephen Greenblatt and Jonathan Dollimore, for example:

> There were some in the Essex faction who saw in the theater the power to subvert . . . in 1601 . . . someone on the eve of a rebellion thought the play sufficiently seditious to warrant squandering two pounds on the players, and the Queen understood the performance as a threat. (Greenblatt, *The Power of Forms in the English Renaissance*, 1982)[5]

> A famous attempt to use the theatre to subvert authority was of course the staging of a play called Richard II (probably Shakespeare's) just before the Essex rising in 1601. (Dollimore, *Political Shakespeare*, 1985)[6]

Dollimore's introduction proceeds to celebrate the fact established by this 'famous attempt' that 'literature was a practice which intervened in contemporary history in the very act of representing it' – a central tenet of materialist criticism.[7] Neither of these critics argues that Shakespeare was a radical playwright (indeed their criticism often positions him as an upholder of the status quo, his plays ultimately 'containing' any subversive impulses they unleash); both rather locate 'the power to subvert' in the appropriation and actual staging of *Richard II* by elements hostile to the crown. According to Greenblatt, the Queen's anxiety about the performance was occasioned by 'something else' beyond and additional to the playtext: a text contains no 'stable core of meaning', rather, its 'shifting meanings' are governed by 'the genre it is thought to embody, the circumstances of its performance, the imaginings of its audience'. Ironically, this new historicist argument comes dangerously close, at times, to reinforcing the view of Shakespeare's play as a hymn to Tudor order: 'that whole may provide a perfectly orthodox celebration of legitimacy and order, as measured by homilies, royal pronouncements, and official propaganda'.[8] I would, however, wish to acknowledge more radical meanings secreted, and waiting to be activated, in the playtext itself; indeed, it is only by ignoring the 'just' assertions of the heterodox voices liberally punctuating at least half of *Richard II*, and by turning a deaf ear to the burning political issues of the late sixteenth century, that such a position could be tenable at all. But let us explore the complex reasons underlying *Richard II*'s 'power to subvert', its particular seditious charge, circa 1601.

The political potency of the 'tragedy' of King Richard has

already been established; he emerges from most Tudor histories as the epitome of tyrannical majesty as defined here by Sir Thomas Smith in his political treatise *De Republica Anglorum* (1583):

> both in Greeke, Latine, and English a tyrant is counted he, who is an evill king, and who hath no regard to the wealth of his people, but seeketh onely to magnifie himselfe and his, and to satisfie his vicious and cruell appetite, without respect of God, of right or of the law.[9]

As we have seen, through the course of the sixteenth century Erasmian humanism gave a new impetus to the Platonic ideals of balance, temperance, and bridled appetites; and this, together with the political struggles of the reformation, encouraged an increasingly less tolerant attitude towards absolutist-style behaviour in rulers. It was not long before particular monarchs were being smeared with the disfiguring brush of tyranny: notably, Mary Queen of Scots who was savagely rebuked – John Knox castigated the 'monstrous regiment of women' – and eventually beheaded for her alleged 'wicked appetites'.[10] Elizabeth Tudor did not, however, escape undaubed, though any criticism of the more powerful English monarch had to be far more covert. The use of analogies to Richard II was one avenue for indirect criticism, and it seems to have been fairly liberally used.

Even Elizabeth's supporters were not averse to using the Richard model to invigorate their warnings, especially about her failing to give ear to their sound counsel. A relative of the Queen, Sir Francis Knollys, wrote a letter to her secretary in January 1578, complaining:

> For who woll persiste in gyvinge of safe counsayle, if her Majestie woll persiste in myslyking of safe counsayle? Nay who woll not rather shrynkingly (that I may say no worse) play the partes of King Richard the Second's men, then to enter into the odious office of crossing of her Majesties' wylle?[11]

Urging that her majesty's safety was being compromised by her 'wylle', Knollys asked for his letter to be shown to the Queen. Indeed, Elizabeth's nearest kinsman, Henry Carey, also saw fit to apply the analogy when Leicester's power was at its height and he felt neglected and passed over by his monarch; he bitterly jibed, 'I was never one of Richard II's men'.[12]

As Elizabeth's reign wore on, and especially in the last decade of the sixteenth century, criticism of her rule extended well beyond court bitchiness about favourites, centring on the explosive issue of succession. Elizabeth had not only failed to marry and produce an heir, but she was also obstinately refusing to name her successor. The discontent of many of her subjects, together with the broad spectrum of their grievances, is rendered apparent in a tract written by her godson, Sir John Harington. Alluding anxiously to the 1590s as 'such a tyme, when malcontentes so abound in citie and countrie', Harington's *Tract on Succession* proceeded to list their gripes: 'that a few favorites gett all, that the nobilitie is depressed, the Clergy pilled and contemned, forraine invasions expected, the treasure at home exhausted, the coyne in Ireland imbased, the gold of England transported, exactions doubled and trebled', concluding on the depressed note that 'all honest hearts' were 'troubled'. Harington laid particular emphasis on the problem of the Irish expenses, unguardedly lamenting the stratagems the Queen found herself embroiled in such as borrowing 'coyne of hir poore subjectes in England without purpose ever to pay it agayne'. Sources close to Elizabeth had also complained as early as the mid 1570s about her 'letting of the realme to farme', and, as a 'landlorde', alienating the hearts of her subjects.[13] All this seems light years away from Dover Wilson's myth of Tudor obedience, harmony and gratitude. Indeed, the charges against Elizabeth had grown unsettlingly close to those used to oust her royal ancestor, Richard II, from the throne.

Unsettlingly close, too, for Shakespeare not to have experienced a certain amount of trepidation about the particular arrangement of negative princely ploys which his play structured around its wayward absolute monarch in 1595 (when the play was first performed):

> RICHARD We are inforc'd to farm our royal realm,
> The revenue whereof shall furnish us
> For our affairs in hand.
> . . . .
> For we will make for Ireland presently.

> (I. iv. 45 – 52)

> GAUNT Landlord of England art thou now, not king

> (II. i. 113)

NORTHUMBERLAND The king is not himself, but basely led
  By flatterers;
. . . .
ROSS The commons hath he pill'd with grievous taxes,
  And quite lost their hearts. The nobles hath he fin'd
  For ancient quarrels and quite lost their hearts.
WILLOUGHBY – And daily new exactions are devis'd.
  As blanks, benevolences, and I wot not what –
  But what a God's name doth become of this?
. . . .
ROSS The Earl of Wiltshire hath the realm in farm.
WILLOUGHBY The king's grown bankrout like a broken man.
NORTHUMBERLAND Reproach and dissolution hangeth over
  him.
ROSS He hath not money for these Irish wars,
  His burthenous taxations notwithstanding . . .

(II. i. 241–60)

Towards the end of her reign, Elizabeth's sick reputation shared
much in common with Richard's: she was accused of pandering
to flatterers, of exacting burdensome and unjust taxes (the years
1592–3 were particularly noted for oppressive taxation), of
farming the realm, and of draining the state's coffers (especially
through her costly and inept Irish policies). Like Richard she
suffered the 'guilt of kindred blood' through slaying her cousin,
Mary – an action which could be interpreted by her detractors as
evidence of an increasing tendency towards tyranny, and which
Richard II might allude to obliquely in the garden scene (see ch.
1, p. 12) – and furthermore, like Richard, she was childless. Shakespeare's play dwells particularly conspicuously and lengthily on
its Queen's barrenness: pregnant with 'nothing', the only heir
Richard's consort will give birth to is her prophecy about 'sorrow's
dismal heir' – Bolingbroke (II. ii. 63). This both jars with Gaunt's
earlier pronouncement about England as 'this teeming womb of
royal kings' (II. i. 51) and fulfils his prophecy about the entropy
inherent in Richard's intemperate behaviour: 'Light vanity, insatiate cormorant,/Consuming means, soon preys upon itself' (II.
i. 38–9). The 'teeming womb' of 'this scept'red isle' has been
rendered void, heirless, burnt out, by Richard's 'rash fierce blaze
of riot' (II. i. 51, 40, 33).
  Elizabeth's sensitivity about her lack of heirs and the anxieties

about succession, and claims to the royal throne that this encouraged, was such that she forbade all discussion of the matter.
As Sir John Harington described, the matter raised fears in the
Queen's mind about her own safety: 'A strong impression remained in her mynde, that if she should allow and permitt men
to examine, discusse, and publishe whose was the best title after
hirs, some would be ready to affirme that title to be good afore
hers.'[14] To allude in the 1590s, to England as a once 'teeming
womb of royal kings' was hardly, therefore, tactful; and that some
dissatisfied with the Queen were all too aware of the incongruity
between Gaunt's encomium and the reality of their monarch's
barrenness is suggested by a passage in a city pageant written
shortly after her death and designed to welcome King James into
the City of London on 15 March 1603. *The Magnificent Entertainment*, by the playwright Thomas Dekker, has the personification
Genius voice a eulogy to James and the City which reverberates
with echoes from Gaunt's famous 'scept'red isle' speech in
Shakespeare's play (II. i. 31–68):

> I am the places Genius, whence now springs
> A Vine, whose yongest Braunch shall produce Kings:
> This little world of men; this precious Stone,
> That sets out Europe: this (the glasse alone,)
> Where the neat Sunne each Morne himselfe attires,
> And gildes it with his repercussive fires.
> This Jewell of the Land; Englands right Eye . . .[15]

Dekker, a committed Protestant who along with many others saw
the Scottish monarch as the best hope for the maintenance and
expansion of the reformed church in Britain and, indeed, in
Europe, celebrated James as a fertile patriarch: note the '*now
springs/A Vine*' which highlights James's fecundity in contrast
with his predecessor. In his pamphlet of 1603, *The Wonderful Year*,
Dekker made the same point about 'Our fruitful sovereigne'
several times: 'The losse of a Queene, was paid with the double
interest of a King and Queene. The Cedar of her goverment which
stoode alone and bare no fruit, is changed now to an Olive, upon
whose spreading branches grow both Kings and Queenes'.[16]
Criticism of the old monarch is contained in this lavish praise of
James, whose coronation had, according to this political tract,
secured a peaceful future for Britain, warding off the threat of civil

strife and of invasion by a foreign Catholic power. Interestingly, too, Dekker refers to Elizabeth in this same pamphlet as 'the great Landlady', drawing out the analogy between her and the notorious monarch-landlord, Richard II, and thereby obliquely denigrating the old Queen. The anonymous play *Woodstock*, about Richard II and his evil counsellors (probably written slightly earlier than Shakepeare's play), had made much of its misled monarch's activities as landlord of the realm, five times stressing this point through its speeches. It would seem that in the 'imaginings' (to use Greenblatt's term in *The Power of Forms*) of many of Dekker's contemporaries, and particularly of radical Protestants of his persuasion, Elizabeth I had been extensively cloned with her tyrannical landlord forebear.

Undoubtedly, the events surrounding the Essex rebellion had rendered the Richard II–Elizabeth analogy more potent by the early seventeenth century than it had been in 1595 when *Richard II* was first staged. However, that Shakespeare's play and Richard's story as it tells it had special topical appeal and commercial value in the late 1590s is suggested by the publication of three quartos of the playtext within the space of two years (Q1 1597, Q2 and Q3 1598); no previous Shakespearean playtext had proved so popular. Furthermore, that some material in the play was considered too politically sensitive to be printed in Elizabeth's lifetime is attested by the excision from these first three quartos of the spectacular 'deposition' scene (IV. i.) which appears in the quartos of 1608 and 1615 and in the First Folio of 1623. Whether or not this controversial but highly theatrical moment of the play was actually staged in the 1590s, or considered too risky by the players, or too subversive by the Master of the Revels who was the licenser and censor of all this period's plays, is open to question; indeed, it is quite possible that the scene was played in some performances (such as the eve of the Essex rebellion) and omitted in others – there is simply no way of knowing.

A key event which increased the 'power to subvert' of Shakespeare's play from 1599 (with or without the contentious 'unkinging' scene) was the publication of a book by the historian Sir John Hayward with the evasive and long-winded title: *The First Part of the Life and Raigne of King Henrie the Fourth Extending to the end of the first yeare of his raigne*. Masquerading as a history of Henry IV (probably to deflect the attention of the censors), this is, in fact, predominantly another tale of Richard, but a particularly subversive one – Hayward was incarcerated in the Tower on its account. It shares with Shakespeare's play an unusually hybrid and sometimes contradictory configuration of the episodes and ethical debates surrounding the circumstances of Richard's nemesis. Indeed, parts of Hayward's book are so similar to Shakespeare's play that the likeness has prompted a chicken and egg argument – which was written first, which influenced which? Apart from the fact that the book was published four years after the play was first staged – strongly indicating it was the egg – Hayward's account is written in a strangely flamboyant and immediate, dramatic style with more dialogue than one would expect from a prose history, suggesting to me that the historian drew on Shakespeare's highly successful play and not vice versa. Consider this passage from Hayward's history depicting the 'scene' between King Henry and his treacherous cousin Aumerle, for example: 'With a confused voice and sad countenance, casting down his eyes as altogether abashed, partly with feare of his daunger, and partly with shame of his discredit; he declared unto the King all the manner of the conspiracie. The king . . . with gracious speeches . . . comforted the Duke'.[17]

Inevitably the similarities between the book and the play led to a certain amount of conflation and confusion in some Elizabethans' minds. This probably accounts for why the trial testimony of Gilly Meyricke on February 17 refers to the play as 'of King Henry the Fourth, and of the killing of Richard the Second, and played by the Lord Chamberlain's players';[18] similarly, Sir Edward Coke, the Crown prosecutor, called it 'a play of Henry the 4th'. By contrast, the actor representing the Lord Chamberlain's company in this trial, Augustine Phillips, who would have been much more likely to accord the play its correct designation, described it as 'of King Richard II'.[19] That the distinction between the two was in danger of being eroded altogether at crucial points in the trial proceedings is illustrated by this indictment against the arch conspirator Essex:

Essex's own actions confirm the intent of this treason. His permitting underhand that treasonable book of Henry IV to be printed and published; it being plainly deciphered, not only by the matter, and by the epistle itself, for what end and for whose behalf it was made, but also the Earl himself being so often present at the playing thereof, and with great applause giving countenance to it.[20]

In the light of the testimonies surrounding the performance the day before the failed rebellion, the play said to have been so fulsomely applauded by the Earl of Essex was almost certainly that acted by the Lord Chamberlain's players – Shakespeare's *Richard II*.

But what was so inflammatory – so 'treasonable' – about Hayward's history that it managed to transmit its powerful charge to Shakespeare's 'stale' play in the circumstances of 1601? The work's epistle dedicatory to the Earl of Essex provided the first bone of contention. Written in obscure, tortuous Latin with a short phrase in Greek, the epistle is nothing if not lavish in its praise of Essex – a 'most illustrious companion', 'the best and noblest of men', 'notable for every virtue'. Furthermore it predicts a glorious future for the Earl, drawing explicit parallels between him and Bolingbroke and shockingly describing the usurper as 'our beloved Henry'. Further incriminating itself in the events it foreshadowed, the text's Preface to the Reader went on to assert how Histories (such as, by implication, itself) provided precepts and 'lively patterns, both for private directions and for affayres of state'. In essence, Bolingbroke the deposer is made to prefigure Essex in this work which represents the usurper as a chivalric, popular hero; and as the people's choice to replace 'dissolute and uncontrouled' Richard: 'The onely man upon whom all men resolved, was Henry Duke of Hereford . . . not at his owne motion or desire, but because hee was generally esteemed meet: as being of the Royall bloud, and next by descent from males to the succession of the Crowne: one that made honourable proofe of his virtues and valour'.[21] It is instructive to compare this description with that of the military hero, 'the general of our gracious Empress' (V. 30), Essex, returning from Ireland in Shakespeare's *Henry V* of 1599. Essex's analogue (foregrounded by the Chorus) is England's darling, Henry V, beloved of the people and 'free from vainness and self-glorious pride;/Giving full trophy, signal, and ostent/Quite from himself, to God' (V. 20–22) – the Christian prince desired of Erasmus.

By the late sixteenth century the Earl of Essex does seem to have had a strong popular and noble following, but the increasing strength of that seems to have been matched by the Queen's growing antipathy towards him. Elizabeth's venom was probably justified. Essex was fashioning himself as the flower of the nobility and gentry of England and as a militant Protestant champion (he favoured an anti-Spanish European coalition); furthermore, as a descendant of Thomas of Woodstock (the murdered Duke of Gloucester, sixth son of Edward III) he had a solid blood-claim to the English throne and, in fact, shared the noble lineage of Bolingbroke. If this was not enough to arouse Elizabeth's suspicion about his grand designs, he was letting it be known that he had lost faith in the Queen's unnatural female magistracy: he told the French ambassador that the faults of the English court proceeded 'chiefly from the sex of the Queen'. When rebuked for his failure to respect adequately Elizabeth's status as God's representative, Essex responded with phrases reverberating with echoes of Erasmus and Buchanan: 'What, cannot princes err? Cannot subjects receive wrong? Is an earthly power infinite?'[22] It would appear that some years before the attempted coup d'état, Essex was shaping himself as the just usurper, an upholder of the people's rights and of the law, whilst supporting constructions of his monarch as a fickle, cowardly Richard II type. His followers, among them Thomas Hayward, were obviously keen to help disseminate these myths, and it is in this light that we should respond to Hayward's history.

The Historie of Henry IV proved immensely popular, selling 500–600 copies (according to its publisher) within the first three weeks of its appearance, and before the Archbishop of Canterbury's order to cut out the dedicatory epistle glorifying Essex was enforced. Hayward was arrested a few months after his book was published, and interrogated by Chief Justice Popham who demanded to know:

> What moved him to set down . . . that the subjects were bound for their obedience to the State, and not to the person of the King?
> What moved him to maintain with arguments never mentioned in the history, that it might be lawful for the subject to depose the King, and to add many persuadings in allowance thereof?
> What moved him to allow that it is well for common weal that the King was dead?[23]

Hayward confessed to inserting these Buchanan-type assertions into his history; and that he had invented a dialogue to show that the subject was not bound in loyalty to the person of the prince, but only to the state. Buchanan's book purveying these views had, we should recall, been officially banned in England as potentially subversive.

Hayward was also charged with collapsing history to make Richard II's time seem like the 1590s, thereby obliquely criticizing the Queen and her counsellors: 'the Doctor selected a story 200 years old, and published it last year, intending the application of it to this time, the plot being that of a King who is taxed for misgovernment, and his council for corrupt and covetous dealings for private ends'.[24] But perhaps the most dangerous charge against him – to which he confessed – was that he had inserted stories, articulated by the Archbishop, to prove that the deposers of princes had experienced good success.

It is hardly surprising then, that Her Majesty was moved to confide in Sir Francis Bacon that she thought this history 'a seditious prelude to put into the people's heads boldness and faction'.[25] Neither is it at all strange that – in what has become in modern times a rather clichéd and quite likely fictitious exchange between Elizabeth and the antiquarian lawyer William Lambard on 4 August, 1601 – whilst perusing various parcels of documents, 'her Majestie fell upon the reign of King Richard II, saying, "I am Richard II, know ye not that" '.[26] By the second half of 1601 the Queen had ample reason to identify with her troublesome ancestor. Furthermore, during Essex's trial the Queen's trusted counsellor, Robert Cecil, foregrounded the dangerous analogy, alleging, 'He [Essex] would have removed Her Majesty's servants, stepped into her chair, and perhaps treated her like Richard II'.[27]

Although Shakespeare's play contained none of the subversive interpolations of Hayward's text it was rendered guilty by close association, and, indeed, by the conspirators obsession with it; but – and importantly – none of the Lord Chamberlain's players was severely punished for involvement in the production on the day before the uprising. Whilst there is evidence that the conspirators feasted eagerly on the play, finding something in it to urge them on to their subversive act, there is none to suggest that the performance of 7 February, 1601 incited the general populace to side with a usurper and rebel against their anointed queen – indeed, quite the reverse. Crowds seem to have gathered in the streets to observe the spectacle of Essex and his men progressing through London intent on their coup d'état, but the escapade met with little popular support; it amounted to a miscalculated dismal failure with dire consequences for its chief perpetrators.

This is not to deny or underplay a 'power to subvert' in Shakespeare's play; but the effect is surely far more subtle, long-term, and ultimately more enduring than that of a play inciting its audience to take to the streets in opposition to their government. It is about challenging the status quo and allowing suppressed and marginal voices to be heard; about interrogating beliefs and offering alternative values; about providing a space for people to imagine differently. The political significance of staging the deposition and killing of a king in the 1590s, for example, lay not in the play's explicit approval or condemnation of it – it does neither – but rather in the offering of it as a real possibility, with a historical precedent, in the wake of absolutism; and the impact of the spectacle itself should not be under-estimated. Such a spectacle was, of course, to be transferred from the stage to the scaffold on 30 January 1649 when Charles I was beheaded for his alleged tyranny and crimes against the people.

As the Middle English poem *Richard the Redeless* makes clear, the idea that forcible resistance to unjust monarchs could be 'just' and even divinely sanctioned was not new to the English in the sixteenth century. Thomas Aquinas himself had sanctioned it in certain circumstances. It was, in fact, the shere weight of Tudor (and subsequently Stuart) propaganda deployed to underpin an increasingly absolutist government that managed to convince people otherwise. Anti-absolutists found a powerful model to challenge Tudor and Stuart so-called orthodoxy in the Richard II story; and, as the following passage from a Civil War polemic foregrounds, Richard II's deposition and killing provided an important precedent for action in the 1640s: 'It has been the custom of our Ancestors to give great reverence to good kings, but the oppressors of the people were secured from doing further mischief by deposing, after which death followed immediately, as in the case of Richard the second . . . that kings may be deposed, is cleer by the forementioned precedent' (1648). The 1640s spawned numerous pamphlets comparing Charles I's reign with Richard II's ('We may apply the mythologie unto our present distractions', 1642); and arguing that the present monarch was even more degenerate than his ancestor ('this kings whole raign hath been a continued Tyranny', 1648).[28] These polemics generally conclude by rejoicing in the positive outcome of the earlier monarch's deposition – God was clearly on the just deposer's side.

The model was again called into play in the politically turbulent 1680s which culminated in the deposition of James II. One famous incident was Nahum Tate's attempt to stage a version of Shakespeare's *Richard II* on 14 December 1680: considering the play too politically dangerous, the Chamberlain stopped the performance. Undeterred, Tate changed the locus of action and its title (to *The Sicilian Usurper*) and it was performed twice in January 1681 before the authorities saw through its disguise and banned it. In a subsequent period of political unrest, Lewis Theobald produced yet another heavily adapted version of *Richard II* which did manage to escape censorship, opening on 10 December 1719 at Lincoln's Inn Fields.[29]

The road to deposition and reformation of the monarchy and government in the sixteenth and seventeenth centuries was a long and tortuous one which required many deeply entrenched values to be dug up along the way, and the seeds of alternative visions to be sown: there can be no doubt that refashionings of Richard's potent tragedy, such as Hayward's history and Shakespeare's *Richard II*, played a crucial part in this process, helping to shape history in the act of representing it.

3

Unstable Signs

The particular pleasure and vitality associated with Renaissance literary forms, especially the drama, has been linked in recent years to the highly unusual set of social and cultural circumstances which gave birth to them – to 'an exceptional, fleeting phase of English history'. In *The Intellectual Origins of the English Revolution* (1965), the Marxist historian Christopher Hill described this pre-revolutionary moment as characterized by the 'confusion and ferment' of its intellectual life, when 'the vision of reality that had supported the rational consciousness for a thousand years was fading'. Building on perceptions such as this, and tuning into a certain radical fervour – an admiration for a world turned upside down in a state of flux, upheaval, and promise – an increasing number of literary critics have attributed the 'cultural revolution' which gave rise to an extraordinarily rich phase in the history of English theatre to the instability and hybridity of the early modern era. Kiernan Ryan has described, for example, how, poised between 'two great epochs', neither feudal nor bourgeois, yet containing the structures and forms of both ('early capitalist society coalescing within a moribund feudal world'), this 'liminal phase' of English history generated vibrant imaginative writing reflecting the 'hybrid, unresolved quality' of an age cast adrift from its old moorings and searching for new meanings, and infused with the drive to 'resist the constraints imposed on expanding desires by the given structures of power'.[1] As this chapter will explore, delineations such as Ryan's certainly help us to account for the preoccupation with unstable signs (words, codes, symbols), the contradictions and paradoxes, and the willingness to challenge conventional wisdom and boundaries, which characterize, and help render aesthetically satisfying, much of Shakespeare's writing, and in particular *Richard II*. Here, as Catherine Belsey has argued, 'the issue is meaning'.[2]

PLAYING AND LAUGHING

Theatrical meaning, and the effect of a production on the imaginings of its audience, have, of course, to do with far more than simply words on a page: how those words are spoken and the silences, expressions, gestures and stage positions which accompany them are crucial; acting techniques, structural implications and spectacle all contribute to the meaning of the narrative they articulate – theatrical sign systems are highly complex. The potential of a play either to consolidate orthodox values or to assist in their subversion cannot, therefore, be assessed solely by focusing on its language: we must, for example, consider the implications of its visual and generic codes too.

As I foregrounded towards the close of the last chapter in relation to the staging of deposition, the role or agency of theatrical spectacle in shaping human consciousness should not be underestimated; the fascinating research of social anthropologists published throughout the 1970s and 1980s has served to heighten modern critical awareness of this. In 'Centers, Kings, and Charisma: Reflections on the Symbolics of Power' (1983), Clifford Geertz described, for example, how ritualistic phenomena can function to unravel as well as sustain the workings of power:

> ceremonies . . . formalities, insignias, stories, etc. mark the center and give what goes on there its aura of being not merely important but in some odd fashion connected with the way the world is built; yet the very thing that the elaborate mystique of court ceremonial is supposed to conceal – that majesty is made, not born – is demonstrated by it.[3]

In this view, staging majesty engaging in its various strategies for consolidating its power (as much Renaissance theatre did), helps to demystify it, revealing its constructed rather than natural basis: playing majesty is thus a politically charged thing to do. Simply through, in Stephen Orgel's words, 'making greatness familiar', its mystique and power can be undermined (something which King James worried about in *Basilicon Doron*, 1599, a treatise of advice for Prince Henry, fearing that it nourished rebellions); but, as we shall see, the act of stimulating laughter at greatness is yet more charged.[4]

Although these critical insights appear to have been lost somewhere along the route to the twentieth century, they were familiar fodder to Renaissance readers fed on a diet of Erasmian humanism in their grammar schools. We have already seen how Erasmus's texts repeatedly emphasize the role-playing, the theatricality, they associate with 'sham' princes, but in his popular satirical work the *Praise of Folly* (1611), behind the distancing mask of the persona Folly, Erasmus went a step further, making much of the potential of theatre itself 'to spoil the illusion':

> If anyone tries to take the masks off the actors when they're playing a scene on the stage and show their true natural faces to the audience, he'll certainly spoil the whole play . . . the king of a moment ago is suddenly . . . the slave, while a god is shown up as a common little man. To destroy the illusion is to ruin the whole play, for it's really the characterization and makeup which hold the audience's eye. Now, what else is the whole life of man but a sort of play? Actors come on wearing their different masks and all play their parts until the producer orders them off the stage, and he can often tell the same man to appear in different costumes, so that now he plays a king in purple and now a humble slave in rags. It's all a sort of pretence, but it's the only way to act out this farce.[5]

Through the course of the sixteenth century the notion of life as a play, the world as a stage, became clichéd to the verge of monotony, and nowhere more so than on the stage itself. As this extract makes clear, Renaissance theatre specialized in the transgression of sartorial codes: an actor (who might well have humble origins) could represent a king, slave and god through a simple change of costume (many of the theatre's critics objected to it on these grounds, arguing that a low-born man should not prank it as a king). Furthermore, if the illusion of the scene was somehow destroyed, hierarchical relations in the play of life might take on a new aspect too, as 'a sort of pretence' – social distinctions might be revealed as, in Geertz's terms, 'made not born'.

These are, of course, just the sort of effects that Shakespearean theatre appears to achieve so effortlessly, though, not surprisingly, a finely tuned artistry can be shown to be at work here. *Richard II*, for example, employs skilful metadramatic techniques to shuffle its audience between the states of absorption and detachment, conviction and scepticism, necessary first to blur the boundaries between the stage and the real world – to create the illusion of life – and then to pierce through the veil of that illusion revealing, in the process, the constructed nature of roles in both spheres. Metadrama is a theatrical style which continuously reflects upon its own artifice, upon the play as a play and upon the business of acting and the rhetorical density that accompanies playing. For example, at crucial points in *Richard II* – often scenes heavy with pathos – the spectators are stimulated to recognize majesty as a rehearsed production. Thus, gazing up at the tragic sight of the defeated sun-king on the battlements, York ponders 'Yet looks he like a king' (encouraging the audience to scrutinize Richard and ask what a king should look like); and then proceeds 'alack, alack for woe/That any harm should stain so far a show!' (III. iii. 70–1). The effect of this scene will depend entirely on its direction and on how the king is portrayed but I would envisage him decked out like a 'pageant' prince, desperately wielding his crown and sceptre in an effort to convince himself and others that he is still fit for the part. Indeed, Richard's speeches make him seem curiously self-conscious and insecure about his role as king, and the tragic brevity of this part. At one juncture he even seems to have forgotten that role and exclaims perplexedly, 'I had forgot myself, am I not king?' (III. ii. 83). Shortly afterwards he reflects how Death allows a king 'a little scene,/To monarchize, be fear'd, and kill with looks' (III. ii. 164–5), simultaneously foregrounding life as a play and the play of majesty. Again, in the pivotal deposition scene, Richard's words draw the audience's attention to his role-playing when he protests that he has not yet had time to learn the part of a subject: 'I hardly yet have learn'd/To insinuate, flatter, bow, and bend my knee' (IV. i. 164–5).

The speeches of others reinforce the life-stage analogy but in humorous contexts. Thus the doddering and foolish York informs his 'unruly' gossip-hungry wife:

> As in a theatre the eyes of men,
> After a well-grac'd actor leaves the stage,
> Are idly bent on him that enters next,
> Thinking his prattle to be tedious;

Even so, or with much more contempt, men's eyes
Did scowl on Richard.

(V. ii. 23–8).

In the scene portraying the York dynasty (the Duke and Duchess, and Aumerle) engaging in a farcial parody of kneeling and begging pardon from the new king, Bolingbroke's words highlight the intentional comedy of this interlude, exclaiming: 'Our scene is alt'red from a serious thing,/And now chang'd to "The Beggar and the King"' (V. iii. 77–8). The playwright seems determined to make the audience recognize and laugh at this burlesque of nobility, this sending up of the rituals associated with nobility and majesty. The same effect – of making greatness and its codes appear ridiculous – is achieved by the gage-throwing scene (IV. i) in which one by one the petty feudal lords add their gauntlets of 'valour' to a veritable heap piling up on the stage floor. The ludicrousness of the spectacle is underpinned by the language: 'If that thy valour stand on sympathy,/There is my gage, Aumerle, in gage to thine' (Fitzwater, IV. i. 33–4).

In spite of many statements to the contrary (Anne Barton, for example, has argued that this play 'has almost no comedy'), and numerous critical assurances that this is the most stately and formal of Shakespeare's plays, *Richard II* contains a great deal of comedy, even farce, intermingled with tragedy and the interrogation of highly serious themes. Furthermore, it is riddled with the forms, and infused with the mocking spirit, of what the Russian thinker Mikhail Bakhtin identified as the 'carnivalesque' in Renaissance literature. In *Carnival and Theatre*, Michael Bristol provides a useful introduction (quoting from Bakhtin's *The Dialogic Imagination*) to Bakhtin's notion of carnival:

> Carnival [is] a 'second life' or 'second culture' sustained by the common people or plebeian community throughout the Middle Ages and well into the early modern period. During the Renaissance, this culture engages with and directly opposes the 'official' culture, both in literature and in the public life of the marketplace and the city square . . . The genres of literature become 'Carnivalized', their structures 'permeated with laughter, irony, humor, elements of self-parody, and finally – this is the most important thing – Carnival inserts into these structures an indeterminacy, a certain semantic open-endedness'.[6]

In the Middle Ages carnivals were associated with festival days (like Shrove Tuesday), when a figure known as the King of Misrule would organize a day of entertainment and feasting involving whole communities dressing up in costumes and masks and taking part in processions, competitions – often tournaments – and farcical plays involving mock trials, crownings and un-crownings and mock killings. It was a day of inversion, of topsy-turveyness, when for a brief space a lowly herdsman might dress up in his feudal master's sumptuous clothes and be royally feasted by him; on such days a beggar could become a king, however transitorily.

Many of the structures of carnival which emerge in *Richard II* should at this stage be apparent but they need some elaboration. They include the tournament referred to by Mowbray in the language of carnival as 'This feast of battle with mine adversary' (I. iii. 92); the uncrowning of Richard and the killing of this King of Misrule; and the social substitutions: for example, in the third act Richard proposes to exchange the trappings of majesty (jewels, sceptre, gay apparel, etc.) for those of an almsman (III. iii. 143–75), and when he is 'unkinged' he informs the spectators observing this 'woeful pageant' that he has 'Made glory base, and sovereignty a slave' (IV. i. 251). As in the *Praise of Folly*, which Bakhtin designated 'one of the greatest creations of carnival laughter in world literature', 'the king of a moment ago is suddenly . . . the slave'.[7] The tensions at the heart of carnival are, in fact, the tensions which pervade *Richard II*: between stability and subversion, between order and disorder, between decay and renewal, between rule and misrule, and between figures like the lean and fasting Lenten Gaunt and the 'insatiate . . . consuming' carnival king of surfeit, Richard. Gaunt's lengthy playing upon his name and evocation of the forms of carnival at the opening of the second act ('And therein fasting hast thou made me gaunt./Gaunt am I for the grave, gaunt as a grave, II. i. 81–2) surely functions to foreground the carnival 'second life' context of *Richard II*. But why is this tragedy so riddled with carnivalesque forms and idiom, and why did Shakespeare deliberately draw attention, early on in the play, to this mocking level?

A simplistic answer would be that he sought to entertain his audience and not pitch them into an unremitting slough of despond: the mingling of serious and gay modes undoubtedly helped achieve this. A Bakhtinian analysis would, however, be rather more subtle. For one thing, carnival was not a politically neutral form: real carnivals were often associated with outbreaks of violence like the famous Shrove Tuesday riots in London; and, as a modern editor of the *Praise of Folly* sees fit to remind the twentieth-century reader, a real threat to the religious establishment emerged from Erasmus's text – carnival and its parodic literary analogues had a propensity to destabilize, to undermine the status quo. For one thing, if carnivalesque modes forced an awareness that social roles were 'made not born', they also prepared peoples' minds for change: if we are all playing roles we might play different, better ones than those allotted to us. As Bakhtin argues, the principle of laughter and the carnival spirit

> leads men out of the confines of the apparent (false) unity, of the indisputable and stable . . . It frees human consciousness, thought, and imagination for new potentialities. For this reason great changes . . . are always preceded by a certain carnival consciousness that prepares the way.[8]

The carnivalesque like so many other techniques in this play, in fact, encourages its audience to eye things 'awry' (*OED*: 'away from the straight'), to view aristocracy and majesty in a parodic, alternative light. As Bakhtin stresses: 'laughter has a deep philosophical meaning . . . It is a peculiar point of view relative to the world: the world is seen anew (and perhaps more) profoundly than when seen from the serious standpoint'. Eyed through the carnival lens there is a certain natural inevitability about the substitution of a King of Misrule by one of rule and order, about change and renewal, which has profound political implications. From the Bakhtinian perspective the warped vision carnival affords is invigoratingly 'utopian [in] character and oriented toward the future'.[9] This certainly seems applicable to a play which helped prepare the way for the deposition and killing of a king and the increasing democratization of government half a century later.

SETTING 'THE WORD ITSELF AGAINST THE WORD': UNDOING WORDS

If *Richard II* subjects medieval and Renaissance rituals and visual

37

signs of greatness to radical scrutiny, unravelling and exposing the symbolic codes of nobility and kingship precisely as codes, it achieves a remarkably similar effect with verbal signs, destabilizing the familiar and relentlessly thwarting our attempts to tie meanings down. In fact it does this so skilfully and so thoroughly that several critics have located something resembling a twentieth-century postmodernist enterprise at work in this play: its early modern author verges on becoming a type of Derridean 'avant la lettre', a precocious deconstructionist. Among the most accomplished and convincing of such analyses is Catherine Belsey's 'Making histories then and now: Shakespeare from *Richard II* to *Henry V*'. According to Belsey's argument:

> The beginning of *Richard II* seems rooted in the simple unity of names and things, but the plays chart a fall into differance which generates a world of uncertainties. The issue is meaning . . . Read from a postmodern perspective, they reveal marks of a struggle to fix meaning, and simultaneously of the excess which necessarily renders meaning unstable.[10]

The origins of this theoretical approach can be traced to the work of the Swiss linguist Ferdinand de Saussure (1857–1913). Challenging the traditional referential view of language – that words stand for things, that meanings are fixed – Saussure proposed a radical alternative: that a word is a verbal sign with two sides, an acoustic image or sound pattern and a concept (or, if written down, a visual 'signifier' and a meaning, the 'signified'), and that the connection between the two is arbitrary. The link between signifier and signified is actually a convention agreed by all users of a given language. Jacques Derrida's theory of deconstruction built upon Saussure's model: signifiers can never have settled signifieds; language is a system of 'differences' and not an aggregation of units of meaning – words only mean what we think they do because of their relation and difference to other words. If we apply this to Shakespeare's play, we might locate a traditional view of language in Gaunt who insists that his name matches his state exactly; whilst Richard's arbitrary use of language – the way he manipulates words and breaks cultural conventions to get his own way and fulfil his own desires – seems to foreground the instability of the sign associated with deconstruction, and to initiate 'the fall into differance' and 'uncertainties' that Belsey finds in *Richard II*: linguistic and political instability do appear to coincide in this play.

Certainly, too, a self-conscious rhetorical density and wordiness – the 'excess which . . . renders meaning unstable' – are features of *Richard II*.[11] Indeed, the very fact that the play is written entirely in verse undermines our attempt to understand it prosaically; and, as we might expect of poetry, words are deployed in startlingly novel and thought-provoking ways. *Richard II* weighs, measures and tastes words ('grief boundeth where it falls,/Not with empty hollowness, but weight', I. ii. 58–9; 'How long a time lies in one little word!', I. iii. 213; 'your fair discourse hath been as sugar', II. iii. 6); gives substance and shape to abstract concepts like 'grief' and 'care'; and regularly negates and empties words linked to concrete things, denying them substance ('unfurnished walls', 'unpeopled offices', 'untrodden stones'). In a witty reversal of this latter strategy, Richard populates his lonely prison cell with the verbal signs of his thoughts (V. i). Through such techniques the boundaries between internal and external categories (the spiritual and the worldly, for example) are broken down, and what constitutes 'reality' is called into question. Additionally, the play assesses and draws attention to the power and currency inscribed in signs ('such is the breath of kings', I. iii. 215; 'Thy word is current with him for my death', I. iii. 231); and to the states which enhance their impact ('the tongues of dying men/Inforce attention', II. i. 5–6; 'they breathe truth that breathe their words in pain', II. i. 8). Words are even instructed to arm themselves (III. ii. 86), can be fought with (III. iii. 131), can be lost (III. iii. 145), sought after (II. iii. 71), become 'tormentors' (II. i. 136) as well as comforters (II. ii. 76), can be companions (I. ii. 55), and can be hoarded (I. iii. 253), valued (II. iii. 20), and transported (II. iii. 81). The tendency for them to be misconstrued is also repeatedly foregrounded ('Mistake me not, my lord, 'tis not my meaning', II. iii. 74), heightening audience awareness of the insecurity of signs and their potential not only to be misread but also to mislead.

Indeed, from this perspective it is highly significant that the most consummate juggler with words in this play is King Richard, whose self-reflexive, ironic wit resembles that of the late-sixteenth-century sonneteer. We might think for example of Sir Philip Sidney's brilliant sonnet sequence *Astrophil and Stella*, written in the 1580s, and suspect that Richard's parting words to his queen (who has just greeted him with his negation: 'thou King Richard's tomb,/And not King Richard', V. i. 12–13), 'Tell thou the lamentable tale of me', contain a conscious echo of Astrophil's melodramatic plea to Stella:

> Then think, my dear, that you in me do read
> Of lover's ruin some sad tragedy:
> I am not I, pity the tale of me
>
> (Sonnet 45, ll. 12–14)

It is no coincidence that whilst Sidney's Astrophil has been designated the first deconstructive lyric persona in the sonnet's history, Shakespeare's *Richard II* has received similar attention from deconstructionist critics: the way Richard and Astrophil play with words and meanings is remarkably similar. Indeed, rich with paradoxes, puns and 'traductio' (using a word repeatedly in several cognate forms), forcing attention on the wordishness of words, the instability of language, and the text's own artifice, Shakespeare's play occupies the same linguistic-poetic niche as the Renaissance sonnet. Undoubtedly, this was a clever commercial ploy on the part of the playwright: *Richard II* was written and launched into the marketplace at the height of the vogue for sonnets in England. Yet this play's complex verbal gymnastics has to do with far more than the marketplace, and if we approach it from too postmodern a perspective we run the risk of losing sight of early modern ones: the significance of the sacramental nature of language, for example, tends to be obscured in deconstructionist accounts. As we shall explore in the next section, in Shakespeare's version of Richard's 'tale' the King repeatedly sets his word against the Word of God, his law against the Law of God, with disastrous consequences. Recourse to Renaissance theories of language and 'right' government, to the intertextual network in which it was situated in its own time, can illuminate this oblique aspect of *Richard II* with far more clarity than the deconstructionist's modern perspective glass.

NAMES, SHADOWS, WORDS AND ACTS

In the third book of *The Governor*, detailing the 'incomparable virtue called justice', Sir Thomas Elyot warns his noble reader:

If thou be a governor, or hast over other sovereignty, know thyself
. . . know that thou art verily a man compact of soul and body, and
in that all other men be equal unto thee . . . Thy dignity or authority
. . . is but a weighty or heavy cloak . . . And from thee it may be
shortly taken of him that put it on thee, if thou use it negligently . . .
Therefore whiles thou wearest it, know thyself, know that the name
of a sovereign or ruler without actual governance is but a shadow,
that governance standeth not by words only, but principally by act
and example . . . In nothing but only in virtue ye are better than another
inferior person.

In Elyot's uncompromising view, a sovereign's name is illusory
and meaningless – a mere 'shadow' – unless his acts befit the true
meaning of his name, unless his words match his deeds. 'Vain or
inordinate jangling' – a symptom of intemperance – is unsuited
to 'majesty'; and self-knowledge together with the exercise of
reason are essential precursors of 'the knowledge of justice'.[12]

It is surely no coincidence that Shakespeare's play about the
meaning of kingship and just rule (the dominant themes, it should
be recalled, of the Renaissance 'mirrors' for princes) so relentlessly
explores the relation and interrelations posited in this highly
popular English 'mirror', between names, shadows, words and
acts, and the stability of government. In fact, the play unequi-
vocally divides its two kings and their supporters into distinct
types of speaker from the outset. Thus Bolingbroke repeatedly
emphasizes (five times in the first scene), and establishes it as a
point of honour, of religion, and of right, that his words match
his acts:

> for what I speak
> My body shall make good upon this earth,
> Or my divine soul answer it in heaven.

(I. i. 36 – 8)

> What my tongue speaks my right drawn sword may prove.

(l. 46)

> By that, and all the rites of knighthood else,
> Will I make good against thee, arm to arm,
> What I have spoke.

(l. 75–7)

Look what I speak, my life shall prove it true.

(l. 87)

> by the glorious worth of my descent,
> This arm shall do it, or this life be spent.

(l. 107–8)

Bolingbroke's apprehension of deeds and words appears similar to that of his father, Gaunt, who famously maintains that his name – the sign representing him – fits his composition exactly. Later in the play, deprived of the external codes of his noble status (his lands, possessions, and his imprese), the crucial signs that remain to connote Bolingbroke's nobility are those which cannot be visualized: 'men's opinions and my living blood' (III. i. 26). Shadowy internal things in the end prove of more substance and value to this king in the making than the 'shows' of nobility. Bolingbroke's 'virtue' (evidenced in men's opinions) ensures that he is never, in reality, 'nothing' (see Elyot quote above): his deeds and his spiritual qualities, rather than his name and its trappings, underpin his reputation.

By contrast his enemy, Richard's henchman Mowbray, is most concerned to preserve the signifier of his noble status, his name: his reputation (as opposed to his deeds) is everything, and without that he is, effectively, nothing ('reputation – that away,/Men are but gilded loam, or painted clay', I. i. 178–9). Mowbray exists in a world of externals and empty words, and the penalty for that is shown to be dire: with his banishment his voice, and the power inscribed in its noble English strains, will be silenced for ever: 'The language I have learnt these forty years,/My native English, now I must forgo'; 'you have engaol'd my tongue'(I. iii. 159–60, 166). In this play those who put gaps between words and deeds, between their words, the law, and the Law of God, ultimately lose the 'currency', the 'sterling' value of their voice, and with it their power.

Richard is, of course, the prime example of a word and law breaker in *Richard II*. Violating, at every turn, agreed cultural, religious, social, and legal conventions – the traditions which determine and stabilize meanings and maintain the status quo in language, the law, and in power relations – Richard, who has made the mistake of imagining he is the sign of signs, the maker and not the subject of law – is himself eventually broken, emptied of meaning, and silenced for good. The most unambivalent example of Richard's flouting of the law in this play is his seizure of his cousin's lands and possessions, his failure to acknowledge Bolingbroke's 'rights and royalties' (II. iii. 119) following Gaunt's death. Both York and Bolingbroke foreground the injustice and the potential for social disruption inherent in Richard's flagrant breach of the law. York challenges Richard:

> Take Herford's rights away, and take from time
> His charters, and his customary rights;
> Let not to-morrow then ensue to-day:
> Be not thyself. For how art thou a king
> But by fair sequence and succession?
>
> (II. i. 195–9)

Power is provisional, it depends on the maintenance of the symbolic system – if custom is breached, the whole system of stable relations is undermined and threatened with collapse. Bolingbroke's words reinforce this crucial point:

> Wherefore was I born?
> If that my cousin king be King in England,
> It must be granted I am Duke of Lancaster
> . . . .
> I am a subject,
> And I challenge law . . .
>
> (II. iii. 121–133)

What Richard has singularly failed to understand, and what Bolingbroke is fully cognizant of, is that the king's law becomes meaningless if the king flouts it. The destructive qualities associated with Richard's law-breaking are inherent in the build-up of 'un' words throughout this play. Indeed, the theatrical structures of *Richard II* do seem to strive to underpin the same perspective as Elyot's 'mirror' – that virtuous deeds, not names and jangling words, are the true signs of kingship. Richard's poor grasp of reality, his absorption in externals and empty words is highlighted by his own ludicrous and pathetic call to arms:

Is not the king's name twenty thousand names?
Arm, arm, my name! a puny subject strikes
At thy great glory.

(III. ii. 85–7)

Lacking (in Elyot's terms) 'virtue' and 'governance', Richard is
reduced to a 'name' – the empty sign of kingship, a 'shadow' –
and shortly that name as well as his office is 'taken of him' because
he has worn his authority 'negligently' (see Elyot quote above).
Signless and evacuated of meaning, Richard is finally 'nothing':
'King Richard's tomb,/And not King Richard' (V. i. 12–13).

THE BRITTLE MIRROR

Yet is he? Many influential critics including the Arden editor
Peter Ure, and Anne Barton, have implied otherwise, seeing a
positive development in this tragic hero's character – a type of
spiritual renewal – which stems from the densely emblematic
mirror-breaking episode (IV. i). Ure has described how this scene
'acts as a pivot in the transformation of Richard from self-conceit
to humility, from King to Man . . . to a person tragically aware
of his ordinary humanity'.[13] In fact this puzzling scene, riddle-like
in its complexity, brings the oblique play of sacramental language
throughout *Richard II* sharply into focus; but, I would argue, its
dextrous arrangement of theatrical material defies our attempts
to fix its meanings. Again, in order to appreciate the rich
complexities and resonances of this episode recourse to other
Renaissance texts is essential.

In the Renaissance a glass or mirror was densely symbolic. It
could be a flattering glass, representing a Narcissus-like self-
obsession, with connotations of vanity, luxury, lust, deception,
superficiality, pride, and vain glory. Alternatively it could be a
glass of self-awareness, reflecting divine light from the soul and
representing the opposing values of prudence, wisdom, purity,
and truth. Interestingly, and importantly, mid-sixteenth-century
Protestant theatre, drawing closely on Calvinist theology in *The
Institution of Christian Religion*, had fostered the use of mirror
imagery for another, related purpose – to signify and teach God's
Law, synonymous with the biblical Word. Thus, for example, in
Lewis Wager's play *The Life and Repentance of Mary Magdalene*, (*c.*
1550) Mary's spiritual regeneration is assisted by a personification

of the Law who (in relation to the man 'dronke and blynde in his owne love') instructs her:

> Wherefore as I sayd to a glasse compared I [the Law] may be,
> Wherin clerely as in the sunne lyght,
> The weaknesse and sinne of himself he may se,
> Yea and his own damnation as it is ryght.
> . . . .
> So the lawe is like a certaine looking.[14]

Protestant theatrical tradition had established God's Law, then, as like looking in a glass, as 'a certaine looking'. By the late sixteenth century, striving to see from different perspectives – as *Richard II* badgers its spectators to do – had well-established religious, truth-telling implications.

All the above mirror symbolism can be located in the brittle glass episode of Shakespeare's play – the playwright, like his tragic protagonist, wittily juggles words, but his purpose appears to be the confounding of any easy, straightforward, superficial vision: this play's deeper realities seem to reside beneath the opaque surface of the text, among its shadows. Dense with irony and contradictions, the mirror scene is, in fact, extraordinarily difficult to analyse but let us try to unravel and decode at least some of its layers.

With the bullying Northumberland standing over him demanding that he read out the list of his 'grievous crimes', unkinged Richard calls for a mirror, declaring that there:

> I'll read enough
> When I do see the very book indeed
> Where all my sins are writ, and that's myself.

> (IV. i. 273–5)

Essentially, Richard's request is absurd because the mirror is merely a material sign representing abstract ideas – a symbol – and symbols should not be read and deployed literally as he intends to do – the gesture is histrionic in the extreme, yet we cannot ignore its sacramental implications. 'The very book indeed' is unmistakably the Bible – the book of the Law – which (if it were that and not just a mirror) might bring Richard to a closer awareness of his sins. Another floating, peripheral meaning is the one mentioned in the first chapter – the 'mirrors' for princes (truth-telling advice books). Yet both these meanings are undermined by the strategically placed comma – Richard himself is the book. This could imply that Richard is going to turn his eyes inward to view the state of his soul (a worthy spiritual enterprise resonant with the injunction: 'Know thyself'), but the claim is rendered highly problematic because Richard might also be suggesting (defiantly) that he is the law. In fact, the 'mirrors for princes' have a great deal to say about kings taking it upon themselves to represent the 'living law'. For example, self-consciously echoing Aristotle, Plutarch, Cicero and Suetonius (a formidable list of authorities), Erasmus declares: 'A good, wise, and upright prince is nothing else than a sort of living law'. However, we know that Richard is none of these things, and resembles more Erasmus's 'tyrant': one who 'sets up laws . . . and all things sacred and profane to his own personal preservation or else perverts them to that end'.[15] Sir Thomas Smith's political treatise underscores the same point: a tyrant 'breaketh lawes alreadie made at his pleasure'.[16] Drawing attention to the crucial bond between the law and God's Law, Erasmus upbraids the law-breaker with the diatribe:

> You compel your subjects to know and obey your laws. With far more energy you should exact of yourself knowledge and obedience to the laws of Christ, your king . . . On what grounds, then, do you grant yourself pardon and consider as a matter of sport and jest the countless times you have broken the laws of Christ . . . by whose sacraments you are bound and pledged?[17]

If Richard is representing himself as 'the living law', he is guilty, yet again, not only of arrogance and hypocrisy, but of contravening God's Law in the manner of a tyrant.

Mirror in hand, Richard further compromises himself by dwelling first upon his wrinkles – his external self, not the inner truth. The biblical passage which is crucial here is James 23: 'For if any be a hearer of the word, and not a doer, he is like unto a man beholding his natural face in a glass'. This certainly seems to suit Richard and to confirm him in sin, yet again the vision is complicated because he goes on to pronounce against this flattering glass which has got him into so much trouble. Is he, therefore, gaining greater self-awareness, even seeing his own damnation in the glass? In shattering the mirror, he might be rejecting his former 'brittle', sinful self, and even prophesying his own death (broken glass was an omen of death), thereby acknowledging his humanity; alternatively, or indeed, simultaneously, he could be furnishing Bolingbroke with an emblematic lesson about the fragility and transience of kingship. Certainly if the mirror is read as a symbol of the Law, the spectacle of the king breaking it is highly symbolic in yet another way.

Bolingbroke's response to the gesture and Richard's comment on the 'moral' of this 'sport' (see Erasmus quote above) is similarly weighted with contradictory meanings. 'The shadow of your sorrow hath destroy'd/The shadow of your face' (IV. i. 292–3) might signify that it is only a mirror which has been broken and not Richard's actual face; alternatively it can be read as implying that Richard's sorrow is unreal – mere show – and that his histrionic game has destroyed his shadow (Richard lacks substance, like Elyot's 'shadow' king of 'names'). Richard reads it in yet another way, however, suggesting that his sorrow is 'substantial' and 'lies all within', and that 'these external manners of lament' are the shadows of the grief in his 'tortur'd soul' (IV. i. 293–8): through a deft verbal manoeuvre he asserts the truth of his grief. Essentially, if Bolingbroke's rejoinder was a reprimand (we should recall his earlier insistence that nobility resides in acts not shows), Richard's juggling with shadows has reversed its meaning. Has he really learned a spiritual lesson here as he claims, or is he being sarcastic and merely playing with words again to assert his own will – a sort of witty one-upmanship?

It is not at all clear that Richard genuinely reaches an awareness of deeper 'shadowy' truths through the course of this scene. What is certain is that the episode thwarts our inevitable desire to try to stabilize it: indeed, this play's obsessive confounding of single, straightforward viewpoints should make us extremely wary of tying its meaning down – of asserting its critical 'truth'. Undoubtedly, we would do better to respect the semantic open-endedness of *Richard II* and be content with uncertainties and paradoxes which can, after all, generate a great deal of aesthetic pleasure. Indeed, whether or not Richard experiences a process of spiritual growth at all before his death is highly debatable. We see him in the deeply moving prison scene, for example, continuing to set the word against the word, and seeming unable to make sense of biblical meanings (V. v. 1–66). Although he has been forced to recognize his human vulnerability, and acknowledges that he has wasted time and indulged in profligate behaviour, he clings steadfastly to his 'right' to the throne – a right which is totally dependent, in his eyes, on his anointed status. However, Richard's tormented Christ-like suffering and the extreme pathos of his tragic end serve to maximize audience sympathy for him. If the play leaves us uncertain about Richard's spiritual status, it also refuses to confirm whose side God is on: whilst Providence is implicated in dispersing the army of Welshmen loyal to King Richard (they are misled by conventional signs in the universe into thinking he is dead), we also know that Henry IV's reign was plagued – as Richard prophesies – by Northumberland's rebellion and civil wars. Shakespeare's multifaceted 'perspective vision' of kingship, in fact, functioned to ensure that while supporters of Tudor orthodoxy – of the view that the monarch was above the law because of his divinity – might be sufficiently satisfied with this representation of Richard II that the play would escape censorship, those favouring the heterodox view of 'just' kingship might see much here to gratify their oblique vision of how the truth might be played out on the stage of life sometime in the future.

4

Gender Perspectives

PERIPHERIES AND CENTRES: UNRAVELLING GENDER

'Awry: (*OED*). Away from the straight; to one side; unevenly, crookedly, askew'

It is both very apposite and interesting that the greater truthfulness of 'awry' perspectives is authorized in *Richard II* through a character constrained to peripheral viewpoints – whose social space is 'to one side', in the shadow of her male counterparts, solely on account of her gender. Prior to the dialogue between Queen Isabel and Bushy at Windsor Castle, the audience has seen a fair amount of the King's consort but beyond one brief, 'womanly' line enquiring into her male relative's wellbeing – 'How fares our noble uncle, Lancaster?' (II. i. 71) – Isabel has been a silent witness to troubled scenes at the heart of England's power structure. Appropriately (given Elizabethan norms governing female behaviour), hers has been a vicarious, marginal, and voiceless role in this public hegemonic context: she has quite literally been seen and not heard. Isabel's anxieties and forebodings, are, however, given free expression in the private domestic space in the company of her husband's closest friends; but her unsettling feminine intuitive perspective is immediately undermined and even potentially negated by Bushy's lengthy, riddling exposition of the opposing 'straight' or centric view. Consummately juggling with words and shadows in a manner worthy of Richard, Bushy wilily argues:

> Each substance of a grief hath twenty shadows,
> Which shows like grief itself, but is not so.
> For sorrow's eye, glazed with blinding tears,
> Divides one thing entire to many objects,
> Like perspectives, which, rightly gaz'd upon,
> Show nothing but confusion; ey'd awry,

Distinguish form. So your sweet Majesty,
Looking awry upon your lord's departure,
Find shapes of grief more than himself to wail,
Which, look'd on as it is, is nought but shadows
Of what it is not . . .

(II. ii. 14–24)

Bushy's reasoning is, ironically, very 'askew' and distorting, and definitely not to be trusted. He is effectively counselling Isabel to avoid distinguishing form by not looking 'awry', and to be content with comforting confusion: the equivalent, as one feminist critic has succinctly put it, of telling her 'not to worry her pretty little head with such matters'.[1] The Queen's perspective (importantly construed by her as the prodigy of her 'soul'), is, however, almost immediately validated by the arrival of Greene, bearing news of Bolingbroke's rise, confirming the substance of Isabel's shadowy insights, and – for the audience – the greater veracity of certain de-centred ways of looking. A useful analogy is the sixteenth-century anamorphic painting by Hans Holbein, *The Ambassadors* (now in the National Gallery), viewed from a centric point, the curious structure between the two ambassadors' feet defies our attempts to understand it, viewed 'to one side' the shadowy distorted shape comes into focus and we discern a skull. The Elizabethan observer of this painting would have been aware of the spiritual lesson contained in the awry perspective: the 'memento mori' would remind him that – like these two admirable ambassadors – in the pursuit of worldly ambitions he must not lose sight of more enduring (but less immediately tangible) spiritual goals and truths.

Productive of truer insights awry perspectives may be, yet they are also closely associated in this play with impotence and intense frustration: Shakespeare notably allows the audience to observe Queen Isabel venting her bottled-up exasperation on a gardener – another perceptive character striving to discern the political shape of things from the margins. Significantly, the menial gardener seems to be privileged with even more knowledge of events at the centre than the Queen, who is shown resorting to ignoble strategies like hiding amidst the 'shadow of . . . trees' (III. iv. 25) and eavesdropping on servants' gossip: powerless, voiceless, and humiliated, Isabel is, as she exclaims, 'press'd to death through want of speaking' (III. iv. 72). Importantly, the Queen is not the only female character in *Richard II* to be allotted theatrical – and, therefore, public Elizabethan space – to voice her dissatisfaction with the impotence accorded by her gender role: the Duchess of Gloucester, having unsuccessfully urged her brother-in-law 'To stir against the butchers' of her husband's life (I. ii. 3) begs to know 'Where then, alas, may I complain myself?' (I. ii. 42), only to have her frustration compounded by Gaunt's passive and unsatisfying rejoinder, 'To God, the widow's champion and defence' (I. ii. 43). Grief, sorrow and weeping eyes are the visible expression of unwanted impotence in this play, and both Isabel and the Duchess are portrayed metaphorically drowning in them – a fate which, we should recall, also befalls Gaunt in his illness and Richard after his fall from power and extreme marginalization.

Whilst Queen Isabel and the Duchess of Gloucester stop at pleading with male relatives in their attempts to exert political influence, the Duchess of York – the only other substantial female part in *Richard II* – is depicted taking drastic and decisive action in the face of male rebuttal, with considerable success. Portrayed as an 'unruly' scold, and subjected to York's misogynistic abuse ('foolish woman', 'fond mad woman', 'frantic woman', 'old dugs', V. ii. 80–95; V. iii. 87–8), the elderly and arthritic 'Mrs York' clambers onto a horse, races off to the centre, and actually gets things done: through her actions she compels the King to spare her only son's life. The audience might laugh at her shrewishness (Bolingbroke brands her a 'shrill-voic'd suppliant' of 'eager cry', V. iii. 73), but they can also admire her pluck: indeed, a certain relief is associated with her frantic, productive activity as contrasted with the former excess of female impotent sorrow. The Duchess of York is, in fact, revealed by this play to be surrounded by male 'put down' terms, stigmatized as unruly and a shrew, precisely because she refuses the extreme marginalization and powerlessness that is thrust upon her gender: she speaks and she acts in ways which threaten the patriarchal dominance of the play world and, indeed, of Elizabethan society. Thus her rejoinder to her husband's 'Peace, foolish woman', is, notably, 'I will not peace' (V. ii. 80–81). We might remark at this point how the play appears to be exposing for the audience's perusal – whether or not this was a conscious strategy on the part of the playwright is open to question – how gender roles were constructed and maintained by Tudor patriarchy. This exposure was, in fact, both encouraged and foregrounded by the Elizabethan stage practice of cross-dressing – of women being played by men. The spectacle of a man in drag inevitably invites us to reflect on how gender roles are understood and determined (or 'contructed') by factors extraneous to biological sex: with a little help from make-up, costumes and mannerisms, males can quite convincingly play female parts. Cross-dressing undoubtedly encouraged recognition, therefore, that the female gender role was not 'natural', or 'God-given', as Elizabethan patriarchy proclaimed, but rather shaped by cultural forces and circumstances, in the interest of the prevailing male hegemony. The realization that roles are prescribed and not 'written in stone' is an essential precursor to social change; we might take these deductions a step further, then, and propose that the Elizabethan stage functioned to undermine and destabilize patriarchal assumptions and practices in relation to 'women' simply through exhibiting them.

Yet this play also subjects male roles to radical scrutiny – it 'deconstructs' them – and it achieves this principally through highlighting the considerable distance between male vocalizations about manliness – a frequent occurrence in *Richard II* – and the actual behaviours we see on stage. This effect is reinforced by the 'female' characters overtly commenting on the unmanliness of the men surrounding them and by the women appearing to act more reasonably than men (Elizabethan patriarchy viewed reason as a male attribute). Take the first scene of the play, for example, "Tis not', Mowbray instructs the court in an excess of lofty, hubristic language:

> the trial of a woman's war,
> The bitter clamour of two eager tongues,
> Can arbitrate this cause betwixt us twain.

> (I. i. 48–50)

'Zeal', heat and 'blood' must arbitrate the quarrel between him and Bolingbroke, warring with words is, he maintains, a womanish undertaking. However, the audience only ever gets the opportunity to see the two men doing precisely this – warring with words at great length whilst 'dolled up to the nines' in chivalric, tournament gear: Mowbray's desired 'chivalrous . . .

knightly trial' (I. i. 81) never actually takes place. Surely such boastful pretensions to virility and manhood as Mowbray's and the feudal peers' in the gage scene – effectively another 'bitter war' of 'eager tongues' between men – are being consciously undermined by such theatrical manipulations? Throughout the reign of Queen Elizabeth I, similar scenes took place regularly at court during spectacular ceremonial jousts: knights dressed up in all their machismo finery, strutted around boasting their prowess, but they never actually wounded their opponents. It all amounted to an elaborate, costly and pretentious display of rank and power; but presumably these events were also highly entertaining. Our playwright was undoubtedly casting an amused glance at such courtly rituals; rituals which figures like the Earl of Essex – 'the flower of nobility', 'militant Protestant champion' – regularly participated in. Perhaps we should indulge in a further wry reflection here, recalling how the Earl informed the French ambassador (in an effort to undermine Elizabeth's rule) that the faults of the English court proceeded chiefly from the Queen's sex (see ch. 2, p. 27). It is highly ironical and noteworthy, therefore, in the light of Essex's posturing and the general anxiety surrounding 'unnatural' female magistracy in the late sixteenth century, that, in the courts of Shakespeare's play (Richard's and Bolingbroke's), most of the faults seem to proceed from behaviours constructed by men as effeminate yet enacted by men; the chief example being, of course, King Richard. Indeed, characterized as vain, fashion-conscious, given to jangling words, fickle, wilful, and prone to tearful outbursts, Shakespeare's king is a paradigm of female frailty as shaped by early modern patriarchy.

If Richard was the only example of troubling male 'effeminacy' in this play, we might read this situation simply as the text's reflecting the consistently 'feminine' constructions of this king of misrule in the chronicles, and possibly hinting at Elizabeth's unsound government through the Richard analogy. Yet the unstable representation of gender generally throughout *Richard II* – its regular confounding of gender distinctions as formulated by Elizabethan patriarchy – undermines any such easy assumption. As explored above, Shakespeare's validation of awry perspectives through a female character confers unusual authority on the female voice: according to patriarchal constructions, female voices were naturally more shrill, fond, wavering, foolish, fickle, vain, lascivious, unreliable, unreasonable, and unsound, than men's. When female voices are allowed to be heard in *Richard II* (and, admittedly, this is not often), they are, in fact, accorded greater competency and theatrical 'weight' than those of the male voices with which they engage. Thus, the Duchess of Gloucester's intelligent arguments, her urging of Gaunt to noble, politic and incisive acts following Gloucester's murder, seem impressive juxtaposed to the male inactivity and paralysing reliance on Providence that she is upbraiding. It is remarkably easy, therefore, for the audience to concur with the Duchess's angry assessment of Gaunt's virility:

> That mettle, that self mould, that fashioned thee
> Made him a man . . .
> . . . .
> That which in mean men we intitle patience
> Is pale cold cowardice in noble breasts.

> (I. ii. 23–34)

Twice she undermines his manhood, before branding him a coward: Gaunt's words do indeed seem 'hollow', contrasted with his sister-in-law's 'weighty' grief and the substance of her arguments (I. ii. 59).

A not dissimilar effect is achieved in the more amicable parting scene between Isabel and Richard (V. i). Striving to promote more masculine, lion-like and kingly responses from her 'fair rose', Isabel eloquently urges:

> What, is my Richard both in shape and mind
> Transform'd and weak'ned? hath Bolingbroke depos'd
> Thine intellect? hath he been in thy heart?
> The lion dying thrusteth forth his paw
> And wounds the earth, if nothing else, with rage
> To be o'erpow'r'd, and wilt thou, pupil-like,
> Take the correction mildly, kiss the rod,
> And fawn on rage with base humility,
> Which are a lion and the king of beasts?

> (V. i. 26–34)

Isabel is firmly in control here: the outraged, protective wife takes the flailing husband-king to task, transgressing normative gender boundaries and revealing her superior intellectual strengths and courage, in an all-out effort to save her pathetic, child-like spouse. In short, gender roles are reversed in this section of the scene: Richard, clothed in the signs of manhood, is reduced to subservient wife-child status; Isabel, bearing the outward marks of womanhood in her costume and demeanour (underneath, of course, is a male actor) is, through her commanding, controlling speech, metaphorically 'wearing the trousers'. Yet the effect is more complicated than this because Isabel's words – 'my Richard', 'pupil-like' – construct Richard more as a bullied schoolboy than a woman. Indeed, periodically throughout this play we get glimpses of an immature, petulant, child-like monarch, eager for tales, given to tears, caressing his mother earth and appearing to desire more to be rocked in a peaceful cradle than to exercise monarchical authority over his realm. Landing on the coast of Wales, for instance, he declares:

> Dear earth, I do salute thee with my hand,
> Though rebels wound thee with their horses' hoofs.
> As a long-parted mother with her child
> Plays fondly with her tears and smiles in meeting,
> So weeping, smiling, greet I thee, my earth . . .

(III. ii. 6–10).

Richard's words are confusing – first he caresses 'Dear earth', his mother (earth is traditionally construed in female, nurturing terms), then he appears to be the mother smiling and crying on greeting a 'long-parted child', then once again the appeal to 'my earth' seems to position Richard in the nurtured rather than the nurturing role. The overall effect, taken together with what we see of Richard elsewhere in this play is, I would suggest, to convey the King's pathetic immaturity, his self-centred, centric vision of things – 'my kingdom', 'my earth', 'my gentle earth' – which is in touch with his own needs and desires but devoid of the nurturing capacities and the ability to see things from the perspective of others (including those at the margins of society) so essential to effective leadership. Indeed, this king's exclusively ego-centric view is so extreme as to resemble that of a child who has never grown up – it is incompatible with kingship.

Thus this play shows us a few competent women locked into roles which forbid them centre-stage parts, and several foolish, vain unreasonable men – including King Richard – inhabiting

55

centric roles they are totally unfit for. The external signs of manhood and womanhood are revealed as frequently misleading – women can belie cultural stereotypes and be intelligent and reasonable, men can behave like babes. Furthermore, whilst *Richard II* repeatedly voices conventional patriarchal commitments, it just as frequently subverts them. We would be hard pressed to draw out from this a vision of a misogynist 'patriarchal bard' – as delineated by some feminist critics – sympathetic to the type of extreme gender stereotyping and prejudice articulated here by William Tyndale (*c.* 1530):

> A king that is soft as silk, and effeminate, that is to say, turned into the nature of a woman, – what with his own lusts, which are as the longing of a woman with child, so that he cannot resist them . . . shall be much more grievous unto the realm than a right tyrant. (*Obedience of a Christian Man*)[2]

Tyndale would undoubtedly have concurred with Samuel Taylor Coleridge's equally woman-unfriendly assessment of Shakespeare's monarch:

> [Richard] is weak, variable, and womanish, and possesses feelings, which, amiable in a female, are misplaced in a man, and altogether unfit for a king. (*The Twelfth Lecture*)[3]

Shakespeare shows us a king whose leadership is undermined by the foibles and weaknesses of character his culture located in the construct 'woman'; nevertheless, Richard *is* a man *and* a tyrant; and the implications of this play are that with more positive 'feminine' qualities – namely the ability to see obliquely, and to nurture – both Richard and his realm would have fared better. It is noteworthy in this respect that his deposer, Bolingbroke, is depicted as in touch with the social margins, sympathetic to the needs and desires of the 'common people' (I. iv. 24–36); and, furthermore, as a concerned father who appears to take his nurturing responsibilities seriously (V. iii).

Finally, we can conclude that, in its interrogation of the meaning of kingship, *Richard II* breaks down rigid gender boundaries, problematizes the hegemonic stature of medieval and Tudor patriarchal attitudes, and invites a reassessment of the meaning of 'man' and 'woman' in a changing society struggling to eschew the worst excesses of political tyranny. Political and gender instability, in fact, go hand-in-hand in this play; and the troubling distance between signs and what they represent is once again confirmed as the central preoccupation of *Richard II.*

5

Reinventions

It is, of course, a truism that every generation possesses the history it desires, refashions the past in its own image, reads into it its own prejudices and looks at it from its own peculiar angle of vision . . . what we mean by history is usually the account of our own, national development in a warring world . . . each age interprets the past in the light of its own preoccupations. (John Dover Wilson, 'The Political Background of Shakespeare's *Richard II* and *Henry IV*', 1939)[1]

We find in Shakespeare only what we bring to him or what others have left behind; he gives us back our own values. (Gary Taylor, *Reinventing Shakespeare*, 1989)[2]

The point of Shakespeare and his plays lies in their capacity to serve as instruments by which we make cultural meaning for ourselves. (Terence Hawkes, *Meaning By Shakespeare*, 1992)[3]

At first sight there appears a curious unexpected affinity between the ultra-conservative critic Dover Wilson's astute reflection that 'each age interprets the past in the light of its own preoccupations' and the observations – fifty years later – of the theorists Taylor and Hawkes about how we impose meanings on writings from the past, namely Shakespeare. Indeed, the comparison of these brief excerpts makes Dover Wilson seem like a post-modernist in the wings, yet this would be a gross misconception; if we delve slightly deeper into his essay we uncover a yawning methodological gulf separating him irreconcilably from latter-day theorists.

The provenance of his piece is fascinating and highly relevant: it emerged from a lecture 'delivered before the German Shakespeare Society' in 1939 – the year Germany invaded Poland, plunging Europe into the Second World War. From his podium at the famous poetry centre at Weimar, infused with nationalistic sentiment (which did not preclude a fervent glance at shared Germanic origins), Dover Wilson addressed the assembled brotherhood of Bard worshippers, making a moving appeal for unity in the name of Shakespeare (and Goethe):

> It is a great honour – and a great moment of my life to be standing here . . . and addressing you on the greatest of English poets, the poet this society exists to honour, the poet who unites our two nations in a common allegiance, and will continue to unite them for ever! Political clouds may arise from time to time in the heaven that overarches us both; but such clouds can never obscure the light of him whom Goethe himself hailed as his own 'Stern der schönsten Höhe'.[4]

Dover Wilson's anxious rallying speech was insecurely anchored in the popular humanist misconception that Shakespeare's genius – like all great art – could somehow transcend political differences; a view not dissociated from constructions of Shakespeare as redolent with 'universal truths' for 'all times', yet curiously at odds with Dover Wilson's reflections on history in the same lecture. His address pushed these assumptions a step further, claiming that a shared love of poetry, and in particular of Shakespeare, could exert a powerful unifying influence, to the point where ardent Bardolatry could perhaps even heal political and national rifts and avert war (vestiges of this type of belief still exist and undoubtedly underlay John Major's government's – flag-waving – policy that Shakespeare should, indeed, must, be taught in all British schools). Beneath Dover Wilson's lofty idealistic rhetoric we can, however, detect a sadder, more confrontational rankling: how could a nation so appreciative of Shakespeare – the pinnacle of civilization in his estimation – be on the verge of thrusting Europe into chaos? In fact, this Shakespeare editor pulled out all the Bardolatry stops in his laudable (if far flung and audacious) endeavour to repulse the chaotic tide of war that threatened; and in the course of his campaign *Richard II* emerged in that most influential of its wartime and post-war guises, as a hymn to Tudor orthodoxy.

Dover Wilson's argument revolved around fear of disorder and anarchy: 'all' Elizabethans were terrified of this, he assured his audience – 'it governed men's thoughts'; 'The historical and political thought, then, of Shakespeare and his contemporaries was determined by their fears of chaos and their gratitude to the royal house which had saved England from it'. The Tudor dynasty had rescued England from the horrors of civil war – the Wars of the Roses – which had been initiated by 'the actions of the usurper Henry IV, who was, as the chronicler Hall taught them, "the first author of this division" '; in consequence it was 'incontestable' that Bolingbroke would have been regarded by Elizabethans as one who had merely usurped the throne 'under colour of a process of law utterly illegal', destroying England's 'sanity and health, unity and order'. Furthermore, the Elizabethan's 'only fear' was lest 'something should arise' to threaten the divinely ordained Tudor monarchy which had restored order to the nation – 'order first, liberty afterwards' is this lecture's motto. According to Dover Wilson, Shakespeare's play 'was a mirror' reflecting these universally held beliefs. He concluded his address on the cautionary and revealing note that he hoped he had shown 'that these plays should be of particular interest to German students at this moment of . . . history'.[5]

Dover Wilson thus invited his audience to reflect on the analogies between the events of Shakespeare's play and those that were unfolding in Germany in 1939. Although never mentioned in his address, Hitler emerges from this lecture as an illegal usurping Bolingbroke figure – 'the first author of this division' – threatening to thrust Germany into an epoch of anarchy. Shakespeare, the civilizing force, was effectively being summoned to demonstrate the error of these ways, and to testify to the universal craving of 'thinking' people for order and stability: 'Order, or Degree, is the basis of his political philosophy, as it is of all thinking Elizabethans'.[6] This was of course the basis, too, of the 'Elizabethan World Picture' expounded by Tillyard in 1943 and which underpinned his thesis in *Shakespeare's History Plays*, that 'orthodox doctrines of rebellion and of the monarchy [were] . . . shared by every section of the community'.[7] Writing in 1957, Irving Ribner echoed and reinforced the highly subjective perspectives of these earlier authorities: 'There can be no doubt that Shakespeare believed in these almost universally-accepted doctrines of absolutism and passive obedience'.[8]

The most startling thing to leap from the pages of Dover Wilson's article is his apparent total lack of self-reflexivity: Shakespeare's version of Richard's history may have been embedded in the preoccupations and beliefs of his time, but Dover Wilson's reading of Shakespeare's play was most certainly not. Foregrounding his primary activities as a Shakespearean editor in the opening paragraphs, his writing harnesses an authoritative and truth-telling status for itself which precludes subjectivity or political manoeuvring on the part of the scholar-editor. At no point does Dover Wilson concede that his point of view is shaped by his own fear of disorder and chaos as England stood on the perilous brink of another war. Furthermore, in order to argue his unacknowledged but deeply political perspective on Shakespeare, Dover Wilson is rather more than sparing of the truth, resembling a 'centric' Bushy type who would rather not grapple with oblique perspectives because of the more honest (but troubling) vision they might reveal: he hides, and hides from, the play's disturbingly heterodox voices and structures. The idea that Shakespeare might have dabbled sympathetically with radical viewpoints was clearly too horrific even to contemplate: Dover Wilson's centric view was – in his own words – 'incontestable'. By implication, no other interpretation was possible. But if Shakespeare's text did not support his reading, neither did history: early-twentieth-century historians were aware of, and had documented the debates between absolutists and democrats in sixteenth-century England which did not point to the type of universally held beliefs which Dover Wilson and his followers constantly reiterated. This is not, therefore, a style of criticism respectful of the text and of history, which we would want to emulate.

My lengthy discussion of Dover Wilson's inflammatory but fascinating lecture is not motivated by a desire to demolish, but rather by a wish to illustrate the style of dogmatic, patriarchal literary criticism against which the more theoretically informed and self-aware criticism of the last twenty years or so has tended to react, and in the process to shape itself – sometimes too far in the opposite extreme. For example, Gary Taylor's statement, above, appears to suggest that beyond 'our own values' there are no meanings in Shakespeare – a view which most critics would contest. The meanings secreted in the semantics of a text are not – responsibly – infinitely stretchable. However, reader-response theory, generally, has done much to alert us to our subjective status as literary critics, and to the politics of literary criticism; and it has heightened critical awareness that 'each age interprets the past in the light of its own preoccupations'. Literature, in common with other writings from the past including those penned by literary critics, participates in both reflecting and shaping cultural meanings.

Perhaps the most pronounced and graphic example of the interactive play between Shakespeare, criticism, and cultural meaning is Sigmund Freud's deriving the germs of his theories of the unconscious – so seminal an influence on twentieth-century thought – partly from his readings of characters in Shakespeare's plays – notably, Hamlet. Of course, the roots of psychoanalytic theory can really be traced back beyond Freud, to the Romantics, and particularly to Coleridge who, as we began to see in the last chapter, had a great deal to say about personalities in *Richard II*. In fact, Coleridge was responsible for resurrecting this play after the doldrums it had experienced subsequent to Dr Johnson's damning dictum that it did not 'affect the passions, or enlarge the understanding'. In his 1813–14 Bristol lecture, Coleridge reversed the critical tide by pronouncing *Richard II* to be no less than 'a history of the human mind, when reduced to ease its anguish with words instead of action'.[9] These two responses were obviously critical poles apart but Coleridge's suited the nineteenth century's growing fascination with psychological structures and before long he was able to assert that *Richard II*'s 'popularity' was 'owing, in great measure, to the masterly delineation of the principal character'. Coleridge found in Shakespeare's Richard largely that which, in Gary Taylor's terms, he 'brought with him':

> From the beginning to the end of the play he pours out all the peculiarities and powers of his mind: he catches at new hope, and seeks new friends, is disappointed, despairs, and at length makes a merit of his resignation. He scatters himself into a multitude of images, and in conclusion endeavours to shelter himself from that which is around him by a cloud of his own thoughts. ('The Twelfth Lecture')[10]

Coleridge's obsession with psychology in *Richard II* – in particular with Richard's emotional oscillation and inability to control his feelings – in fact, initiated a long train of criticism (and stagings) which set aside the political concerns of the play in favour of focusing on the delineation of the principal characters and relationships between them.

The most striking thing about this critical strand is how variously Richard's character is read: for example, whilst Swinburne found here an unattractive, 'womanish or semi-virile' creature; the 'fin-de-siècle' poet William Butler Yeats discovered in Richard a 'boy of fine temperament . . . a vessel of porcelain' (a sensitive artistic type like Yeats?) subject to the merciless bullying of Bolingbroke – a 'vessel of clay'.[11] Twentieth-century post-Freudian studies have tended to concentrate on Richard's 'neurosis', his 'regressive, exhibitionist' responses to frustration, his infantilism, self-love, self-pity, 'fantasies of omnipotence' and 'God complex' (his identification with Christ); whilst more recent psychoanalytic readings have explored the presentation of family – in particular father-son – relationships in the play. Again, critical fashions can be observed to be highly responsive to the pre-occupations of the cultural moment, and highly subjective; yet studies like this which focus on 'interiority' have another charac-teristic: they tend to lose sight of the culture which gave birth to the play, and in particular of its 'otherness'. Thus, for example, modern (post-nineteenth-century) sexual categories like 'hetero-sexual' and 'homosexual' are too readily projected back into the Renaissance, and King Richard emerges with 'homosexual' ten-dencies because his friends lured him away from his wife's bed ('Broke the possession of a royal bed', III, i. 13). In fact this is to grossly oversimplify the implications of Bolingbroke's allegations in III. i, which have to do with power relations as much as with sex, for this was a society in which men frequently shared beds with their male friends without being thought 'disfigured' (III. i. 10), and incurring abuse. As recent studies of early modern friendship networks have persuasively demonstrated, this was almost certainly a cultural location where 'passionate male friend-ships, at least among élites [were] one of the linchpins of the complicated system of patronage, faction, protection, and jockey-ing for status and preferment that largely constituted the "governance" of the Renaissance'.[12] 'Who was sharing a bed with whom', in the Renaissance, clearly had enormous political sig-nificancies: to focus within the narrow confines of modern sexualities when interpreting speeches such as Bolingbroke's about corrupting male intimacies is not only anachronistic and reductive, but misses the point.

A further major weakness of psychological studies has been their general neglect of *Richard II* as a Renaissance play. Renaissance drama was not 'naturalistic' in the nineteenth- and early-twentieth-century sense, but predominantly emblematic in the ancient European tradition: playwrights were interested in exploring wider public issues like religion, government and morality; in-depth exploration of character was not a feature of Renaissance dramaturgy – characters tended to be complex types, vehicles for ideas, rather than complex personalities. As Evelyn Albright rightly complained in her masterly exposition of the political context of *Richard II* in 1927 (which initiated a reaction against 'Romantic' readings of the play, and the return of critical considerations of its politics – the other dominant strand of twentieth-century criticism):

> The CRITICS have emphasized the 'romantic' aspects of Shakespeare's work to such an extent as almost to ignore any possible connection of his plays with the people of his day and the problems that occupied their minds. His characters are treated as sheer creations who live in a sort of vacuum.[13]

Indeed, trying to create a wholly naturalistic piece of theatre with in-depth explorations of character out of a Shakespeare play is fraught with difficulties, as Sir John Gielgud experienced in 1929 when he made his debut at the Old Vic in the role of Richard II. Gielgud sought to convey an impression of a character somewhere between Swinburne's and Yeats's delineations: sly, vain, callously indifferent, but 'innately well-bred, sensitive to beauty . . . lonely in his remote position of kingship, young, headstrong'. Yet he found the artificial, 'tapestried' language of the play an obstacle to realism – its constant poetry (and those features which we now think of as constituting metadrama) got in the way:

> Everyone speaks in images, parentheses, and elaborate similes, whether gardeners, exquisites . . . the continually artificial style tends to become somewhat indigestible on the stage, and stands between the audience and their desire to get on more intimate terms with the characters and situations.[14]

Shakespeare, of course, never intended his audience to get on 'intimate terms' with his characters; and this would certainly have impeded his exploration of the politics of kingship which demanded the critical distancing achieved by metadramatic techniques. Similarly, Gielgud found that the quarrel of the peers – the gage throwing scene – ran the 'dangerous risk of seeming ridiculous': to solve what he perceived as a major stumbling block of the play, he advised future directors 'to make some discreet cuts to avoid bathos both here and in the Aumerle conspiracy scenes'.[15] Indeed, it has been common practice for twentieth-century productions to cut the 'ridiculous' scenes which many critics have found misjudged: the idea that Shakespeare intentionally inserted comic episodes in what has been perceived as his most formal play, has been anathema to many. Tastes are, however, changing, and an extremely positive feature of Deborah Warner's 1995 production for the Royal National Theatre – which will be discussed later – was its successful inclusion of the comic scenes, uncut.

Theatrical productions are commercial ventures – tickets must be sold for playing to continue – and as such they must appeal, or at least make some concessions, to prevailing tastes and fashions. Whilst scholarship of playtexts must be respectful of the text's substance, and of history, it would be foolish to tie theatre into a strait-jacket which denied directors and actors licence to cut, adjust, and recreate – effectively to make meaningful and satisfying theatre out of texts now four hundred years old. In order to survive, theatre must be vital and vibrant, not overly precious and fossilized: as the Shakespearean actor Ian Richardson succinctly put it, 'If you enter a choir-boy-filled cathedral atmosphere with Shakespeare, you are going to strangle him out of existence'.[16] Whilst issues relating to the politics of kingship and government as explored in Shakespeare's play remained inflammatorily topical, *Richard II* – when it was permitted to be staged – was guaranteed a lively, interested audience, as these comments on the responses to the play's revival on 6 February 1738 render clear: 'it was greatly distinguished by the particular behaviour of the audience . . . who applied almost every line that was spoken to the occurrences of the time, and to the measures and character of the ministry'. Thomas Davies describes how the Covent Garden audience responded boisterously with 'the clapping of hands and clattering of sticks' to the line 'The king is not himself, but basely led/By flatterers'; and when Ross pronounced 'The Earl of Wiltshire hath the state in farm', the words were 'immediately applied to Walpole, with the loudest shouts and huzzahs I ever heard'.[17] John Rich's production was undoubtedly a commercially motivated venture designed to exploit the interest in a play which was at the centre of a heated controversy about Walpole's Theatre

Licensing Bill. A journal letter (2 July 1737) ridiculing such attempts at censorship (and which resulted in the prosecution of *The Craftsman* and its printer) had made the tongue-in-cheek pronouncement that *Richard II* should on no account be permitted to be staged 'without considerable Castrations and Amendments; for it not only represents an obstinate, misguided Prince depos'd by his people, which is agreeable to the Principles of the Revolution; but likewise contains several Passages, which the disaffected may turn to their Account'.[18] Rich's production was timely in the extreme; however, as the eighteenth century proceeded and the controversies surrounding the English Revolution became confined to history books, and as the power of the monarchy dwindled and people even forgot what 'the divine right of kings' meant, the 'disaffected' increasingly found less in *Richard II* to 'turn to their Account': the play's topicality waned, Johnson told the world it was boring, and productions of it ceased completely. Alternative veins of meaning had to be mined and built upon if Shakespeare's stale play was to be successfully revived.

Romantic criticism – as we have seen – provided a partial answer to the problem: focus could be shifted from the characters as vehicles for the exploration of public themes to characters as vehicles for the exposition of the psyche: Richard the sensitive, poetic tragic hero-king, flawed by his emotional instability, made his stage debut in the mid nineteenth century with Charles Kean's production in 1857 at the Royal Princess's Theatre in London (see Figs. 1 to 3). Involving a cast of hundreds with real horses on stage and a wealth of medieval pageantry, this highly successful reinvention was nothing if not spectacular. Kean's brainchild scored a palpable hit through tapping into two lucrative springs: the nineteenth-century fascination with the mind – and in particular with hypersensitive Byronic types – and the Victorian nostalgia for Gothic artistry, splendour, and ceremony. There were sixteen magnificent scenes, elaborately advertised on the playbill, with sets painted by artists featuring medieval castles, cathedrals, palaces, ruins and dungeons. A 'historical episode' showing Bolingbroke's re-entry into London apparently incorporated a 'Dance of Itinerant Fools . . . as Old as the Reign of Edward the Second' (playbill). Walter Pater's pronouncement on the production testifies to its being a veritable monument to nineteenth-century 'taste':

1. Charles and Mrs Kean as Richard and his queen, Royal Princess's
Theatre 12 March 1857.
V & A Picture Library/Theatre Museum, London

2. Painting of the set for the 'historical episode' showing Bolingbroke's entry into London, Royal Princess's Theatre 12 March 1857.

V & A Picture Library/ Theatre Museum, London

the winning pathos, the sympathetic voice of the player, the tasteful archaeology confronting vulgar modern London with a scenic reproduction, for once really agreeable, of the London of Chaucer. In the hands of Kean the play became like an exquisite performance on the violin.[19]

Pater's accolade of Kean's Richard – the 'graceful, wild creature'at the heart of this 'symphony' – was highly influential, helping to shape Frank Benson's definitive (by all accounts) 'fin de siècle' interpretation of the title role which apparently strove to convey this artist-king's preoccupation with 'perfect expression'. In fact Benson's legendary performance became something of a classic model and a difficult act to follow throughout the first half of the twentieth century, so much so that Gielgud's interpretation of the role at the Old Vic in 1929 was criticized for not placing sufficient emphasis on the artistic side of Richard's nature (Fig. 4). Inevitably, such sympathetic portrayals of the King supplied a fitting context for the development of the 'Tudor Myth': Bolingbroke, the ambitious, calculating, utilitarian bully – Dover Wilson's instigator of disorder – was the natural stage villain to depose Richard the fragile artist – the much-wronged martyr king.

The politically turbulent post-Second-World-War period stimulated a return to an interest in and exploration of the play's political angles, and helped to produce contrasting, far less congenial interpretations of the title role. In a production at Stratford in 1951, Michael Redgrave presented a harsh, refreshingly unsentimentalized portrait of the King, redolent with cruelty, spite, and envy (Fig. 5); but the tide had really turned for Richard in 1962 when, at the American Shakespeare Festival, he was portrayed as an unsavoury gangster lacking the shrewdness and strength essential to the success of his enterprise. Richard's other face – that of the martyr – had not disappeared, however: in David Warner's production in 1962 at Stratford, Richard was presented as undergoing a spiritual transformation, gradually evolving from a monarch of vanity and guile to become a tall white-robed, Christ-like figure. But it was left to the RSC director and Cambridge don John Barton to grapple extensively – though not altogether successfully – with the intellectual and aesthetic complexities of presenting a play about divine right and just kingship to a twentieth-century audience almost four centuries removed from such pressing Elizabethan concerns, and for whom the main attribute of English royalty was now the handbag, not the crown and sceptre.

The academic preoccupations underlying Barton's 1973 Stratford *Richard II* (1974 in London) are particularly well documented because the Shakespearean scholar Anne Richter Barton took part in a recorded discussion about the production in Barton's stead, together with the lead actors Richard Pasco and Ian Richardson, and the theatre scholar Glenn Loney. As Anne Barton described in the introduction to the debate, John Barton had isolated three major problems which any director of this 'most relentlessly Elizabethan' play had to face when staging *Richard II*: first, how to convey the remote idea of sacramental kingship to modern spectators; secondly, what to do to make its formal, stylized verse and complex figurative language more accessible to twentieth-century audiences; thirdly, how to convey the history in which the play is embedded, in particular the tragic, blighted nature of Henry IV's reign – again something which would have been very familiar to Elizabethans, but which is far from commonplace today.[20] As well as addressing these issues, Barton was determined that his production should convey the concept of 'the king's two bodies' (discussed in ch. 1): as Anne Barton related, Ernst Kantorowicz's book of that title had provided the 'germinating idea' underpinning Barton's vision. Taking the concept to its literal conclusion, Barton cast two actors to alternate the parts of Richard II and Bolingbroke on successive nights: Pasco played a sensitive, poetic and pathetic Richard one night, and Richardson played a dangerous, unpredictable, cunning, more masterful Richard the next. Effectively, Barton's *Richard II* reflected the 1960s and 1970s vogue for two contrasting visions of Richard pitted against an ambitious, practical and ruthless Bolingbroke; it is difficult, though, to see how this very literal approach furthered Barton's aim of educating his audience about the Elizabethan commonplace of the king's body natural and body politic being united in one person. Critics were divided about just how much of a gimmick this dual casting amounted to, but most conceded that the superb performances of the two lead actors justified it. Certainly, it must have helped the box-office figures: enthusiastic theatre-goers were compelled to attend twice if they wanted to discourse knowledgeably about the two Richards.

3. Section of playbill advertising the spectacular 'historical episode', Royal Princess's Theatre 12 March 1857. *V & A Picture Library/Theatre Museum, London*

6. John Barton's RICHARD II, Royal Shakespeare Theatre 1973.
Shakespeare Centre Library: Joe Cocks Studio Collection

A panoply of symbolism and special effects were introduced to convey the balanced structure of the play as understood by the director (as one king falls, the other rises), and to emphasize the theatricality of kingship: Barton added a prologue in which the two lead actors were given their parts to play for that night – a shrewd metadramatic technique – and the scene designers Timothy O'Brien and Tazeena Firth created a much-criticized set consisting of two identical ladders separated by a rising and falling platform; there were also actual buckets on stage to provide a concrete illustration of Richard's bucket and well lines (IV. i. 184–9). The director dealt boldly with his audience's lack of historical knowledge about Henry IV's sad, troubled reign and early death by adding some of Henry's lines from 2 *Henry IV* to the end of *Richard II*, and by concluding his production with a tableau of the two kings presided over by Death – the ultimate monarch. In an attempt to overcome his audience's lack of familiarity with Renaissance language and imagery, Barton provided symbolic props as visual analogies for what he perceived as the 'talismanic' words of the play: a dish of soil on the forestage provided Gaunt with some English earth to run his fingers through during his patriotic 'scept'red isle' speech (II. i. 31–68); a snowman gave visual expression to the 'mockery king of snow' line (IV. i. 260); and a variety of hobby horses, from sugar-candy ones at Coventry to sinister black ones on which Bolingbroke's baronial henchmen rode (resembling Tolkien's 'black riders' in *The Lord of the Rings* – a favourite book of Barton's), provided graphic underpinning to the director's colourful, idiosyncratic vision (Fig. 6). Facial masks, together with an alienated mode of speech delivery, served to further accentuate the metadramatic style of the production; and the frame of Richard's shattered mirror was used to full effect: strung around his neck it became a halo, then a noose, and then it resembled a window through which the twin kings perused their mirror image. The Duchess of Gloucester rose from the grave as a ghost to deliver her lines – adding a spooky appeal – and a ghoulish Northumberland paraded around the stage on stilts resembling a vulture. Additionally, many of the speeches in the play were broken up and redistributed – an adaptation which most reviewers found puzzling and rather pointless. Finally, apparently to emphasize Bolingbroke's and Richard's shared tragic fate, Barton replaced the groom who visits Richard in Pomfret Castle with a disguised Bolingbroke: the two kings were construed as fellow victims destroyed by the crown.

As we might imagine, some theatre-goers found this barrage of special effects gimmicky in the extreme: indeed, one audience-participant in Anne Barton's discussion group summed up the experience as 'simply horrendous'. Furthermore, having seen the play, he confessed to being none the wiser about the 'king's two bodies' concept informing the production until enlightened by Anne Barton's introduction. It seems that, for many, the director's laboured attempts to fill in the gaps in the spectators' understanding about Renaissance concepts had met with abysmal failure. In fact, the obsessive thrusting home, through an array of devices, of the point about the shared plights of the two kings seems to have left most spectators under the mistaken apprehension that the two kings were, indeed, mirror images of one another – 'interchangeable', 'essentially the same' – nothing, of course, could have been further from Shakespeare's vision, and from what the Elizabethans understood from their chronicles. Yet this 'generally overstuffed' production appears – from the comments of the reviewers – to have been engaging and at points highly entertaining, though not always for reasons the director intended; as one scholar recalls, for example:

> Not all these devices came off. Richard's cry of surrender at Flint, 'Down, down I come, like glist'ring Phaethon', is a little comic when the descent is made in a goods lift; and the final swish of the murdered King's coffin down the chute was all too reminiscent of the mechanical conjuring tricks of a modern crematorium.[21]

In spite of, or perhaps even because of, its 'gimmicks', Barton's controversial production was clearly experienced as innovative and vibrant, and attracted wide audiences: the combination of the director's vision and the masterful acting of Pasco and Richardson brought the old play to life again, and perhaps the best measure of its success is how influential it proved on subsequent productions.

Barton and the RSC had, in fact, signalled respectability to a rush of imaginative, non-traditional interpretations, predominantly metadramatic in style, and increasingly in tune with a new vogue of literary criticism that was stressing Shakespeare's play-

5. 'Here cousin, seize the crown', Michael Redgrave as Richard and Harry Andrews as Bolingbroke, Shakespeare Memorial Theatre Stratford 24 March 1951.

Photograph by Angus McBean

4. John Gielgud as Richard II, Old Vic, 18 November 1929.
V & A Picture Library/Theatre Museum, London

texts as open-ended unfinished structures written to be performed, reinterpreted, and not preserved in scholar's formalin. Following Barton's lead, a number of directors invented prologues: in Elizabeth Huddle's American Conservatory Theatre production (1982), for example, the whole cast, wearing modern dress, presented a Brechtian-style introduction. Another woman director, Zoe Caldwell, clearly impressed by Barton's emphasis on role-playing, decided to cast three actors as Richards and Bolingbrokes for her production at the Shakespeare Festival at Stratford, Ontario (1979). However, by far the most unusual and visually impressive reinvention of this period was Ariane Mnouchkine's production for the Théâtre du Soleil (1981 in Paris), inspired by the 'kabuki' and 'noh' traditions of Japanese theatre, which culminated in a phantasmagoric tableau of Richard, sparsely clad in a loin-cloth, grappling with Exton's 'ninja' assassins in a bamboo matrix.

In contrast to these highly experimental approaches, the British Broadcasting Company produced a screen version in 1979, directed by David Giles with a star-studded cast including Derek Jacobi, Jon Finch and Sir John Gielgud, which appeared accomplished and 'authentic' to reviewers at the time, but which has since been condemned by some critics – notably, Graham Holderness – for promulgating the conservative, Tillyardian myth of the play's politics.[22] Throughout the 1980s various attempts were made to revivify and render meaningful the more disturbing political veins of the old Shakespearean text; for many directors this meant lifting the play out of its medieval context altogether. Robin Lefèvre's production at the Young Vic in 1981 boldly transferred the setting of the play to Eastern Europe before the Revolution: a dark pit, sloping stage and iron balcony provided the sombre backdrop to a bleak world of frock-coated elder statesmen and booted and darkly uniformed court officials, in which Richard appeared as a Czarist martinet, and Bolingbroke as a red-tied Lenin-like usurper. Michael Bogdanov's *Richard II*, in the Wars of the Roses series at the Old Vic (1989), presented Richard as a languid, velvet-clad regency dandy (in the artistic Bensonian mould), pitting his inadequate wits against a pragmatic Bolingbroke kitted out in a military tunic heavy with gold epaulettes (Fig. 7). In 1990 the RSC with Ron Daniels at the helm took *Richard II* once again into a fascist-Stalinist world of despots and dictators, this time – rather curiously – somewhere in a neo-classical, vaguely Van Dyckish time-warp conjured up by huge white classical columns and noblemen clad in black fur and leather (Fig. 8).

However, the most outstandingly innovative production of recent years was undoubtedly that directed by Deborah Warner for the Royal National Theatre (which opened at the Cottesloe, 2 June 1995), starring Fiona Shaw as Richard II and David Threlfall as Henry Bolingbroke. Critical alarm bells were jangling about this much publicized production long before the preview, but no disaster ensued – far from it. The most pressing concern for critics of the feminist persuasion was inevitably, what would be the effect of casting a woman in the role of a man traditionally characterized as effeminate? Surely this would only serve to reinforce a negative stereotype of woman? I certainly shared this blinkered apprehensiveness but – much to my delight – any misgivings about the controversial casting were dealt a swift blow by an early trip to the Cottesloe to see Fiona Shaw in action. As the *Guardian* theatre critic Michael Billington proclaimed of Shaw in the title role:

> Since intelligence and imagination count for as much in acting as gender, it makes perfect sense for women to play male roles . . . Shaw, with her short cropped hair and white leggings, has an androgynous quality that soon makes you forget the specifics of sexuality. (*Guardian*, 5 June 95)

Here was a Richard the stage had never seen before: neither a languid artist, nor a paradigm of female frailty, nor a cunning coward, Shaw's Peter Pan-like, hopelessly immature boy-king compelled the audience's rapt attention for almost four hours (Fig. 9). To my mind, this was a psychological study ripe for the 1990s of a monarch over-indulged, pampered and pandered to from child-hood – so much so that he was quite convinced of his divinity and untouchability – who had emerged from this aberrant, fatherless upbringing a neurotic, inadequate and lonely individual capable only of game-playing and certainly not adequately equipped to play the arduous adult role of king. In fact history supports such an interpretation: as the programme notes reminded us, Richard was only 10 years old when he was crowned at Westminster. Pathetic but likeable from the first scene, Shaw's Richard sat impishly on his throne, feet dangling unable

7. Tournament scene *RICHARD II*, English Shakespeare Company Wars of the Roses series, directed by Michael Bogdanov, the Old Vic 1989.
Photograph by Laurence Burns

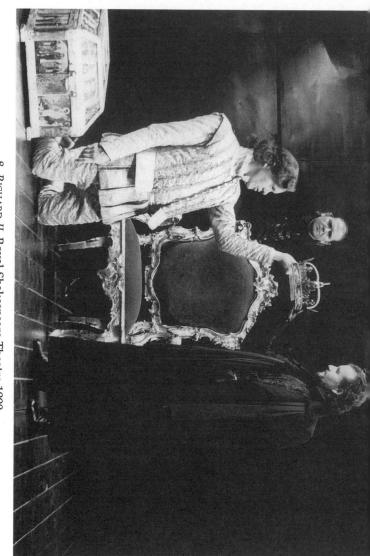

8. RICHARD II, Royal Shakespeare Theatre 1990.
Shakespeare Centre Library: Joe Cocks Studio Collection

9. Fiona Shaw as Richard II, The Cottesloe, the Royal National
Theatre 1995.
Photograph by Neil Libbert

to reach the ground, casting awkward grins at his rout of courtier-friends, fidgeting incessantly and, when standing, shifting nervously from foot-to-foot. Later we saw him sucking his thumb, playing 'horsy' on Aumerle's back, and carrying his crown around in a shopping basket. Gawky, petulant, teasing, exhibitionistic and prone to temper tantrums, Shaw's was emphatically an irresponsible boy-king – there was no sign of a woman's emotions, or of effeminacy here.

Threlfall's Henry was equally unfamiliar, and refreshingly so: here, for once, was a very sympathetic Bolingbroke – a sort of big brother figure anxious to shield his young cousin from blows but keenly aware of the needs of his country and of the importance of justice and just rule. The two cousins cuffed, cuddled, kissed, and generally showed a great deal of affection towards one another, emphasizing this as a tragedy of families, as well as of state: indeed, the whole historical saga emerged from this production as 'a claustrophobic family affair' in which all the combatants were 'intimately, almost incestuously acquainted' (*Sunday Times*, 11 June 95) – an interesting, historically accurate perspective which usually remains undeveloped. Another novel feature was that the Henry of Threlfall's masterfully articulated lines made him the poet-prince of this production; more effectively so because Shaw's breathless, hurried, choppy delivery tended to erase the accomplished virtuosity of Richard's speeches. In their over-keen attempts to create a pragmatic, bullying Bolingbroke out of Shakespeare's text, directors of the last century and a half have been rather brutal in their efforts to nullify the beauty and artistry of Henry's lines, so it was gratifying to see this seemingly relentless trend reversed by Warner.

Another commendable feature was that the play was uncut, leaving its humorous scenes intact and bringing to life aspects of its drama which are frequently neglected: the gage throwing episode added a burst of hilarity to the action as well as revealing the self-righteous barons as ridiculous strutting competitors; and the York family bust-up with Michael Bryant at its centre made for electric theatre. Paola Dionisotti played an impressively strong Duchess of Gloucester upbraiding her cowardly, fatalistic brother-in-law Gaunt (Graham Crowden), and doubling as the shrewish Duchess of York she made the few women in this play a substantial force to be reckoned with. This effect was increased by Brana Bajic's interpretation of Queen Isabel: she played a fitting, astute and caring mother-wife for Shaw's immature, unreasoning king-child. Here then was a long-awaited feminist interpretation of *Richard II* suited to an epoch centrally concerned with the politics of gender; an interpretation which was capable of making its audiences ponder about how gender roles are constructed, and which opened the veins of Shakespeare's text that too often lie untapped – those that undermine male claims to greater competency and reason, and those related ones that cast a sardonic eye at medieval formality and pageantry and the patriarchal structures at the heart of such hegemonic display (structures which persisted in Shakespeare's England).

The set, too, was impressive consisting of a long cruciform space of white and gold which was readily transformed from a medieval gallery, to the scene of a tournament (lined by the audience as if in the lists), to the court. A massive crown positioned centrally above the stage served to remind the audience that this play is – most crudely defined – about power struggles over ownership of the crown and the entitlements that once went with it. Aside from this symbolic gesture, however, the facts of medieval history and politics in which *Richard II* is embedded were neglected, even misrepresented; and perhaps this is where criticism of Warner's production should begin. Whether deliberately or inadvertently, Shaw's Richard showed a marked preference for his cousin Henry over Mowbray in the first scenes, something which is foreign to the playtext and to history; indeed, Richard appeared to stop the tournament because he could not bear to see his cousin hurt. Furthermore, evoking our sympathy from the beginning through his child-like warmth and playfulness, there was nothing about this Richard to suggest his capability for involvement in the type of ruthless cunning and conspiracy implied by Shakespeare's text, and by the chronicles. Equally, the production left me rather uneasy about Isabel's relation with her purported spouse – how on earth could this attractive, intelligent woman be crying her eyes out about this pathetic wimp – unless she *were* his mother, that is. The director's vision, then, was not without its flaws: many critics hated Shaw's thumb-sucking, fidgety king, and several decried the production's apparent lack of interest in the politics of kingship. It is interesting to see how newspaper reviews of this play tended to divide down a left and right approval and disapproval line, with the traditionally conservative papers decrying the performance of the woman in the role of king: 'It's all a ghastly travesty' proclaimed the *Sunday Telegraph* (11 June 95) for example. In a sense, then – and certainly if we care about the politics of gender – this was a highly politicized production, vital and challenging for the 1990s. What more should we ask of a director's vision?

But perhaps one final question should be raised about Shakespeare's. Is it his perfected, unified vision redolent with 'universal truths' that is 'for all times' – as many post-Romantic critics have claimed? Or is it rather that the multifaceted, multivocal and contradictory nature of his vision has enabled directors and actors over the centuries to edit and reinvent, ruthlessly plundering the veins of the old Shakespearean mine they find most lucrative and interesting whilst leaving others sealed or only partially worked, creating meaningful drama for their age out of a rich, but frequently paradoxical, and essentially open-ended form? As I hope this discussion has shown, all the evidence points to the latter: drama is an artistic form restless to be reopened, reworked and highly resistant to closure; thankfully, we may be certain that as long as there is theatre *Richard II* will never be finished.

Notes

CHAPTER 1. POLITICAL VOICES

1. William Baldwin, *A Myrroure For Magistrates*, in *The Mirror For Magistrates*, ed. L. B. Campbell (New York: Barnes & Noble, 1960), II. 31–3, 36–7.
2. Raphael Holinshed, *The Laste Volume of the Chronicles of England, Scotlande and Irelande* (London, 1577), p. 1098.
3. Anon., *Richard The Redeless*, in *The Piers Plowman Tradition*, ed. Helen Barr (London: Everyman, 1993), II. 43, 82–7.
4. Stephen Greenblatt, *The Power of Forms in the English Renaissance* (Oklahoma: Pilgrim Books, 1982), 6.
5. Samuel Daniel, *The First Fowre Bookes of the Civile Wars Between the Two Houses of Lancaster and Yorke* (London, 1595); Edward Hall, *The Union of the Noble and Illustre Famelies of Lancastre and York* (London, 1548).
6. Desiderius Erasmus, *The Education of a Christian Prince*, 1516, trans. Lester K. Born (New York: W. W. Norton & Co, 1968), 173. Hereafter *Christian Prince*. Erasmus believed the 'average prince' of his day needed these 'checks' to stop 'tyranny . . . creeping in'.
7. *Christian Prince*, 152.
8. Quoted in Born's Introduction to *Christian Prince*, 27.
9. *Christian Prince*, 157, 189, 182, 210, 153, 145, 236.
10. *Christian Prince*, 187, 175, 152, 182, 154.
11. Desiderius Erasmus, *The first tome or volume of the Paraphrase of Erasmus upon the newe testament* (London, 1548), sig. Olv.
12. *Christian Prince*, 153.
13. Laurence Humphrey, *The Nobles: or of Nobilitye* (London, 1563), sigs Y5–6.
14. Sir Thomas Elyot, *The Book Named the Governor* 1531, ed. S. E. Lehmberg (London: J. M. Dent & Sons Ltd, 1962), 165, 166, 209. Hereafter, *The Governor*.
15. *Christian Prince*, 156–7.
16. Ernst H. Kantorowicz, *The King's Two Bodies* (Princeton: Princeton University Press, 1957), 25.

17. John Calvin, *The Institution of Christian Religion* (1536; London, 1561), IV.xx.31 f.170v. Hereafter *The Institution*.
18. *The Institution*, IV.xx.31 f.170v–171r.
19. *An Homile Against disobedience and wilfull rebellion*, the first part (London, 1571).
20. George Buchanan, *De Jure Regni Apud Scotos* (1579), trans. Charles Arrowood, *The Powers of The Crown in Scotland* (Austin: University of Austin Press, 1949), 122. Hereafter *De Jure Regni*.
21. Quoted in Conrad Russell, *The Causes of the English Civil War* (Oxford: Oxford University Press, 1990), 131.
22. *De Jure Regni*, 50.
23. *De Jure Regni*, 48–9.
24. Elizabeth I, 'The dowbt off future foes exiles my present joye', in *The Penguin Book of Renaissance Verse*, eds. D. Norbrook and H. Woudhuysen (Harmondsworth: Penguin, 1992), 95.
25. In his treatise about kingship, *Basilcon Doron* (1599), King James railed against the Scottish Reformers with their 'fantasies' about a 'Democratik forme of governement'.
26. *De Jure Regni*, 122.

CHAPTER 2. SHAPING HISTORY

1. State Papers. Domestic Elizabethan. 1598–1601, vol CCLXXVIII, art. 85.
2. Cited in E. K. Chambers, *William Shakespeare: A Study of Facts and Problems*, 2 vols. (Oxford: Clarendon Press, 1930), vol. 2, 326. Hereafter *William Shakespeare*.
3. Sir Francis Bacon, *A declaration of the practises & treasons committed by Roberte late earle of Essex* (London, 1601).
4. John Dover Wilson, 'The Political Background of Shakespeare's *Richard II* and *Henry IV*'. *Shakespeare Jahrbuch*, 75 (1939), 36–51, 40. See also E. M. W. Tillyard, *Shakespeare's History Plays* (London: Chatto & Windus, 1944).
5. *The Power of Forms in the English Renaissance* (Oklahoma: Pilgrim Books, 1982), 3.
6. Jonathan Dollimore, 'Shakespeare, cultural materialism and the new historicism', in *Political Shakespeare*, eds. Jonathan Dollimore and Alan Sinfield (Manchester: Manchester University Press, 1985), 8.
7. *Political Shakespeare*, 10.
8. *The Power of Forms*, 3, 4.
9. Sir Thomas Smith, *De Republica Anglorum* (1583), ed. L. Alston (Cambridge: Cambridge University Press, 1906), Lib. 1, ch. 8, 18.

10. John Knox, *The Works*, ed. David Laing (Edinburgh: The Bannatyne Club, 1846), vol. 1, 411–12.

11. Cited in E. M. Albright, 'Shakespeare's *Richard II* and The Essex Conspiracy', *PMLA*, XLII (1927), 691.

12. Albright, 'Shakespeare's *Richard II*', 691.

13. Albright, 'Shakespeare's *Richard II*', 604, 691, 710.

14. Albright, 'Shakespeare's *Richard II*', 694.

15. Thomas Dekker, *The Magnificent Entertainment* (London, 1604), sig. B1v.

16. Thomas Dekker, *The Wonderfull Yeare* (London, 1603), sig. C1v.

17. Sir John Hayward, *Cotton and Hayward Histories of Henry III and IV* (London, 1642), 123–5.

18. S. P. Dom. Eliz. 1598–1601, vol. CCLXXVIII.

19. Chambers, *William Shakespeare*, vol. 2, 324–6.

20. S. P. Dom. Eliz. 1598–1601, vol. CCLXXV, art. 5.

21. *Cotton and Hayward Histories*, sig. A3r, 117, 130.

22. See Albright, 'Shakespeare's *Richard II*'; and Mervyn James, *Society, Politics and Culture: Studies in Early Modern England* (1986; Cambridge: Cambridge University Press, 1988), 443, 444, 445.

23. S. P. Dom. Eliz., 1598–1601, vol. CCLXXIV, art. 58.

24. S. P. Dom. Eliz., 1598–1601, vol. CCLXXVIII, art. 25, 1.

25. *Sir Francis Bacon his Apologie, in certaine imputations concerning the late earle of Essex* (London, 1604), 10.

26. John Nichols, *The Progresses and Public Processions of Queen Elizabeth*, 3 vols, (1783; London: John Nichols and Son, 1823), vol. 3, 552.

27. S. P. Dom. Eliz., 1598–1601, vol. CCLXXVIII, art. 54.

28. Anon., *The People Informed of their Oppressors and Oppressions With a Remedy against both* (London, 1648), 3, 4; Anon., *The Kings Articles And The Parliaments Honour* (London, 1642), 3.

29. See James G. McManaway, '*Richard II* at Covent Garden', *Shakespeare Quarterly*, 15 (1964), 161–76).

CHAPTER 3. UNSTABLE SIGNS

1. Kiernan Ryan, *Shakespeare* (1989; 2nd ed. Hemel Hempstead: Prentice Hall/Harvester Wheatsheaf) 28–31; Christopher Hill, *Intellectual Origins of The English Revolution* (1965; New York: Oxford University Press, 1982) 7–8.

2. Catherine Belsey, 'Making histories then and now: Shakespeare from *Richard II* to *Henry V*', *Uses of History*, eds. Francis Barker, Peter Hulme and Margaret Iversen (Manchester: Manchester University Press, 1991), 32–3.

3. Clifford Geertz, *Local Knowledge: Further Assays in Interpretive Anthropology* (New York: Basic Books, 1983), 124.
4. Stephen Orgel, 'Making Greatness Familiar', in *Pageantry in the Shakespearean Theater*, ed. David M. Bergeron (Athens, Ga: University of Georgia Press, 1981).
5. Desiderius Erasmus, *Praise of Folly*, 1611 (Harmondsworth: Penguin Books Ltd., 1971), 104.
6. Michael Bristol, *Carnival and Theatre: Plebeian culture and the structure of authority in Renaissance England* (London and New York: Methuen, 1985), 22.
7. Mikhail Bakhtin, *Rabelais and His World*, trans. Helen Iswolsky (Russian ed. 1965; Cambridge, Mass.: The MIT Press, 1968), 14.
8. *Rabelais and His World*, 48–9.
9. *Rabelais and His World*, 11, 33.
10. Belsey, 'Making histories', 33.
11. 'Making histories', 33.
12. *The Governor*, 159, 165–6, 100.
13. Peter Ure, 'The Looking-Glass of Richard II', *Philological Quarterly*, xxxiv (1955), 221.
14. Lewis Wager, *A new Enterlude . . . entreating of the Life and Repentaunce of Marie Magdalene* (London, 1567), sig. E4r.
15. *Christian Prince*, 221, 165.
16. *De Republica Anglorum*, 15.
17. *Christian Prince*, 153.

CHAPTER 4. GENDER PERSPECTIVES

1. Jeanie Grant Moore, 'Queen of Sorrow, King of Grief: Reflections and Perspectives in Richard II', in *In Another Country: Feminist Perspectives on Renaissance Drama*, eds. Dorothea Kehler and Susan Baker (Metuchen, N. J. and London: The Scarecrow Press, 1991), 25.
2. William Tyndale, *Obedience of a Christian Man*, c. 1530, ed. R. Lovett (London: Religious Tract Society, 1888), 93–4.
3. Samuel Taylor Coleridge, 'The Twelfth Lecture', in *Shakespearean Criticism in Two Volumes*, vol. 2, ed. Thomas Middleton Raysor (London: J. M. Dent & Sons Ltd, 1960), 145.

CHAPTER 5. REINVENTIONS

1. Wilson, 'The Political Background', 38–9.
2. Gary Taylor, *Reinventing Shakespeare: A Cultural History from the Restoration to the Present* (1989; London: Hogarth, 1990), 410–11.

3. Terence Hawkes, *Meaning By Shakespeare* (London: Routledge, 1992), 141–53.
4. 'The Political Background', 36.
5. 'The Political Background', 46, 50, 44, 40, 50.
6. 'The Political Background', 40.
7. E. M. W. Tillyard, *Shakespeare's History Plays*, (1944; Harmondsworth: Penguin, 1962) 64.
8. Irving Ribner, *The English History Play in the Age of Shakespeare* (1957; London: Methuen, 1965), 154.
9. Dr Samuel Johnson, *The Plays of William Shakespeare* (1765; New York: AMS Press, 1968), 105; Samuel Taylor Coleridge, *Shakespearean Criticism*, 232.
10. *Shakespearean Criticism*, 146.
11. Algernon Charles Swinburne, *Three Plays of Shakespeare* (New York and London: Harper, 1909), 76; William Butler Yeats, 'Essays and Introductions', in *Discussions of Shakespeare's Histories: 'Richard II' to 'Henry V'*, ed. R. J. Dorius (Boston: D. C. Heath and Company, 1965), 22.
12. Margaret Hunt, 'Afterword', in *Queering the Renaissance*, ed. Jonathan Goldberg (Durham and London: Duke University Press, 1994), 366.
13. Albright, 'Shakespeare's *Richard II*', 686.
14. Sir John Gielgud, 'Stage Directions', 1963, in *'Richard II': Critical Essays*, ed. Jeanne T. Newlin (New York & London: Garland Publishing, 1984), 142.
15. 'Stage Directions', 143.
16. In 'The Royal Shakespeare Richard II', *Staging Shakespeare: Seminars on Production Problems*, ed. Glenn Loney (New York & London: Garland Publishing, 1990), 34.
17. Thomas Davies, *Dramatic Miscellanies*, 3 vols. (London 1783–4), vol. 1, 150–51, 152–3.
18. Cited in James G. McManaway, '*Richard II* at Covent Garden', *Shakespeare Quarterly*, 15 (1964) 161–75.
19. Walter Pater, 'Shakespeare's English Kings', *Appreciations: with an essay on style* (London: MacMillan, 1889), 195.
20. The entire debate is published in Loney, *Staging Shakespeare*, 19–55.
21. Richard David, *Shakespeare in the Theatre* (Cambridge: Cambridge University Press, 1978) 165.
22. See Graham Holderness, 'Radical potentiality and institutional closure: Shakespeare in film and television', in *Political Shakespeare*, 206–25.

Select Bibliography

EDITIONS OF *RICHARD II*

The first Quarto edition of *Richard II* was published in 1597, two more Quartos followed in 1598, another in 1608 (the first to include the deposition scene, IV. i. 154–318), and one in 1615. The First Folio version of the play was printed in 1623. Most modern editions are a collation of Q1 (felt to be close to Shakespeare's manuscript) and F1, with the exception of the Oxford Shakespeare which, usefully, reproduces the F1 version (described by the editors as the most 'theatrical' text), printing the additional passages from Q1 as an appendix.

Ure, Peter (ed.), *King Richard II*, Arden Shakespeare (London: Methuen, 1956; Routledge, reprinted 1994).

Gurr, Andrew (ed.), *King Richard II*, New Cambridge Shakespeare (Cambridge: Cambridge University Press, 1984, reprinted 1995).

Wells, Stanley (ed.), *King Richard II*, New Penguin Shakespeare (London: Penguin, 1969).

Wells, Stanley, and Gary Taylor (eds.), *William Shakespeare: The Complete Works*, The Oxford Shakespeare (Oxford: Oxford University Press, 1988, paperback reprint 1994).

CRITICAL WORKS

Albright, Evelyn May, 'Shakespeare's *Richard II* and the Essex conspiracy', *PMLA*, XLII (1927), 686–720. A masterly exposition: remains a rich repository of useful references for reconstructing the political context of the play.

Barroll, Leeds, 'A New History for Shakespeare and his Time', *Shakespeare Quarterly* 39 (1988), 441–64. Re-evaluating various documentary evidence surrounding the staging of *Richard II* in 1601, this essay challenges new historicist readings of the play.

Bate, Jonathan, and Russell Jackson (eds.), *Shakespeare: An Illustrated Stage*

History (Oxford: Oxford University Press, 1996). A finely illustrated stage history.

Belsey, Catherine, 'Making histories then and now: Shakespeare from *Richard II* to *Henry V*', in Francis Barker, Peter Hulme, Margaret Iverson (eds.), *The Uses of History* (Manchester: Manchester University Press, 1991). Marrying Marxism, deconstruction and historicism in an extremely fruitful way, this is an exciting and important essay.

Bergeron, David M. (ed.), *Pageantry in the Shakespearean Theater* (Athens, Ga.: University of Georgia Press, 1981). Contains seminal essays on the impact of ritual in Shakespeare's drama, including 'Making Greatness Familiar' by Stephen Orgel.

Bristol, Michael, *Carnival and Theatre: Plebeian culture and the structure of authority in Renaissance England* (London and New York: Methuen, 1985). An important study of Mikhail Bakhtin's ideas of Carnival in relation to Renaissance theatre.

Clare, Janet, 'The Censorship of the Deposition Scene in Richard II', *Review of English Studies*, 41 (1990) 89–94. Argues that the deposition scene was probably excised from peformance until after Elizabeth I had died.

Cookson, Linda and Bryan Loughrey (eds.), *Critical Essays on 'Richard II'* (Essex: Longman Literature Guides, 1989). Contains an excellent, accessible essay on the politics of kingship by Raman Selden.

Dollimore, Jonathan, and Alan Sinfield (eds.), *Political Shakespeare: Essays in Cultural Materialism* (1985; Manchester: Manchester University Press, 1994). The introduction, which discusses *Richard II*, is a useful statement of the cultural materialist approach to Shakespeare.

Dusinberre, Juliet, *Shakespeare and the Nature of Women* (London: Macmillan, 1975). Groundbreaking feminist study; identifies Richard as 'one of the few [Shakespearean] men to enter into the experience of women, and discover his nullity in the eyes of the world' (p. 125).

Dutton, Richard, *Literary Lives: William Shakespeare* (Houndsmills: Macmillan Press, 1989). Traces the contexts that produced Shakespeare's writing.

Gilman, Ernest B., *The Curious Perspective: Literary and Pictorial Wit in the Seventeenth Century* (New Haven: Yale University Press, 1978). A useful historical study of the perspective device and the relevance of this understanding to *Richard II*.

Greenblatt, Stephen (ed.), *The Power of Forms in the English Renaissance* (Oklahoma: Pilgrim Books, 1982). Greenblatt's Introduction, which discusses *Richard II*, is a useful starting point for understanding the new historicist approach to the play.

Gurr, Andrew, *Playgoing in Shakespeare's London* (1987; Cambridge:

Cambridge University Press, 1996). A readable account of the theatre and playgoers in Shakespeare's England.

Hamilton, Donna, 'The State of Law in Richard II', *Shakespeare Quarterly*, 34 (1983), 5–17. A good introduction to the Tudor legal debates pertinent to *Richard II*.

Hawkes, Terence, *Meaning by Shakespeare* (London: Routledge, 1992). Explores reader-response theory in relation to Shakespeare

——(ed.) *Alternative Shakespeares*, vol. 2 (London: Routledge, 1996). The introduction is an excellent critical survey of recent debates about Shakespeare.

Holderness, Graham, *Shakespeare Recycled: The Making of Historical Drama* (Hertfordshire: Harvester Wheatsheaf, 1992). Discusses 'chivalry and kingship' and 'patriarchy and gender' in *Richard II*, arguing that Shakespeare's plays offer resistance to forms of ideological dominance like Tillyard's.

Holland, Norman, *Psychoanalysis and Shakespeare* (New York: McGraw Hill Book Company, 1964). A useful survey of psychoanalytic readings of each play.

Kantorowicz, Ernst H., *The King's Two Bodies: A Study in Medieval Political Theology* (Princeton: Princeton University Press, 1957). A classic study: written by a historian, the 'king's two bodies' thesis this expounds, with a chapter devoted to *Richard II*, has proven highly influential.

Kennedy, Dennis, *Looking at Shakespeare: A Visual History of Twentieth-Century Performance* (Cambridge: Cambridge University Press, 1993). A pioneering study of Shakespearean scenography in Europe, Russia, and North America.

Melzer, Annabelle Henkin, and Kenneth Rothwell (eds.), *Shakespeare on Screen* (New York: Neal-Schuman Publishers Inc., 1990). A useful history of screen productions.

Moore, Jeanie Grant, 'Queen of Sorrow, King of Grief: Reflections and Perspectives in Richard II', in Dorothea Kehler and Susan Baker (eds.), *In Another Country: Feminist Perspectives on Renaissance Drama* (Metuchen, N. J. and London: The Scarecrow Press, 1991). A convincing feminist analysis centring on the implications of the perspective device in the play.

Ryan, Kiernan, *Shakespeare* (1989; Hemel Hempstead: Prentice Hall, 1995). A cogent and exciting introduction to radical Shakespeare.

Talbert, E. W., *The Problem of Order* (Chapel Hill: University of North Carolina Press, 1962). Propounds a formidable anti-Tillyardian thesis through a meticulous analysis of sixteenth-century political texts. Sees *Richard II* as a richly equivocal play.

Taylor, Gary, *Reinventing Shakespeare: A Cultural History from the Restora-*

tion to the Present (1989; London: Vintage, 1991). Explores the way each age has refashioned Shakespeare to suit its own ends.

Tillyard, E. M. W. *Shakespeare's History Plays* (London: Chatto & Windus, 1944). A classic study: this conservative, highly influential, interpretation of Shakespearean history should be considered, if only to establish whether all the recent negative criticism of it is justified.

Wells, Robin Headlam, 'The Fortunes of Tillyard: Twentieth-Century Critical Debate on Shakespeare's History Plays', *English Studies*, 66 (1985), 391–403. An extremely useful analysis of this century's debates.

Index

*Recent and
Forthcoming Titles
in the
New Series of*

WRITERS AND
THEIR WORK

WRITERS AND THEIR WORK
RECENT & FORTHCOMING TITLES